English
STEP BY STEP
WITH PICTURES
NEW EDITION

Ralph Boggs

Robert Dixson

PRENTICE HALL REGENTS
Englewood Cliffs, N.J. 07632

Editorial/production supervision and
    interior design: **Tünde A. Dewey**
Pre-Press Buyer: **Ray Keating**
Manufacturing buyer: **Lori Bulwin**
Cover design: **Wanda Lubelska Design**

Illustrations by **Anna Veltfort**

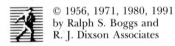
Printed in the United States of America
10 9 8 7 6 5 4 3 2 1

ISBN   0-13-277104-7

Prentice-Hall International (UK) Limited, *London*
Prentice-Hall of Australia Pty. Limited, *Sydney*
Prentice-Hall Canada Inc., *Toronto*
Prentice-Hall Hispanoamericana, S.A., *Mexico*
Prentice-Hall of India Private Limited, *New Delhi*
Prentice-Hall of Japan, Inc., *Tokyo*
Simon & Schuster Asia Pte. Ltd., *Singapore*
Editora Prentice-Hall do Brasil, Ltda., *Rio de Janeiro*

INTRODUCTION

English Step by Step with Pictures was first published in 1956 and was one of the first English as a Second Language texts available. We are celebrating its 35th year with the publication of this new edition.

Any text which can endure the course of three decades, offers an extremely effective methodology to the teacher and student. The popularity of ENGLISH STEP BY STEP stems from the ease with which the instructor can pass on essential grammar and vocabulary to the learner.

Like previous editions, this new edition still contains 45 lessons that present a series of simple, graduated steps designed to give the student a maximum sense of accomplishment. Eight hundred vocabulary words and the essential structures of English are presented and then recycled throughout the text to reinforce learning. To supplement the text there is a workbook available which offers additional written exercises.

In the decade since the last edition, our culture has seen many changes. Hair styles, gender roles, and the demographics of the 1990's are reflected in the updated illustrations of the new edition.

CONTENTS

English STEP BY STEP WITH PICTURES

1 QUESTIONS AND ANSWERS

1. What's this?*
   It's a pen.

2. What's this?
   It's a pencil.

3. What's this?
   It's a computer.

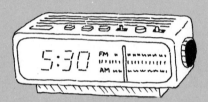

4. What's this?
   It's a radio.

5. What's this?
   It's a table.

6. What's this?
   It's a chair.

7. What's this?
   It's a shirt.

8. What's this?
   It's a suit.

*What's is the contraction of what is.

9. What's this?
It's a dress.

10. What's this?
It's a skirt.

11. What's this?
It's a sock.

12. What's this?
It's a shoe.

13. What's this?
It's a dog.

14. What's this?
It's a cat.

15. What's this?
It's a tree.

16. What's this?
It's a flower.

EXERCISE

Answer the questions in complete sentences.

1. What's this?
   It's a cat.

2. What's this?
   It's a tree.

3. What's this?

4. What's this?

5. What's this?

6. What's this?

7. What's this?

8. What's this?

9. What's this?

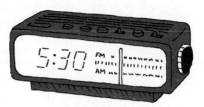

10. What's this?

11. What's this?

12. What's this?

13. What's this?

14. What's this?

15. What's this?

16. What's this?

New Words

a	dog	it	shirt	suit	what
cat	dress	pen	shoe	table	what's
chair	flower	pencil	skirt	this	
computer	is	radio	sock	tree	

2 NEGATIVE STATEMENTS

1. This isn't a sock.*
   It's a shoe.

2. This isn't a radio.
   It's a newspaper.

3. This isn't a table.
   It's a desk.

4. This isn't a shirt.
   It's a coat.

5. This isn't a shoe.
   It's a boot.

6. This isn't a shirt.
   It's a skirt.

7. This isn't a pair of boots.
   It's a pair of pants.

8. This isn't a pair of shoes.
   It's a pair of socks.

*Isn't is the contraction of is not.

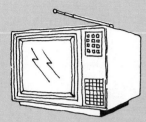

9. This isn't a computer.
   It's a TV.

10. This isn't a desk.
    It's a chair.

11. This isn't a pencil.
    It's a pen.

12. This isn't a chair.
    It's a table.

13. This isn't a school.
    It's a house.

14. This isn't a house.
    It's a school.

15. This isn't a cat.
    It's a dog.

16. This isn't a flower.
    It's a tree.

EXERCISE

Answer the questions in complete sentences. First give a negative answer, and then give an affirmative answer.

1. Is this a pen?
   No, it isn't a pen.*
   It's a pencil.

2. Is this a dress?
   No, it isn't a dress.
   It's a coat.

3. Is this a skirt?

4. Is this a pair of pants?

5. Is this a radio?

6. Is this a shoe?

7. Is this a shirt?

8. Is this a chair?

*It isn't or it's not may be used. It's is the contraction of it is.

9. Is this a dog?

10. Is this a table?

11. Is this a school?

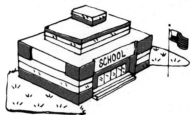

12. Is this a house?

13. Is this a tree?

14. Is this a computer?

15. Is this a suit?

16. Is this a pencil?

NEW WORDS

boot	house	it's	no	pair	school
coat	isn't	newspaper	not	pants	TV
desk					

3 THE INDEFINITE ARTICLE:
A or An

Use *a* or *an* with singular nouns that can be counted:

a pear　　　　*pears*　　　　　　　*an apple*　　　*apples*

Use *a* before a consonant sound: *a pen, a book.*
Use *an* before a vowel sound: *an apple, an orange.*

1. This is an office.

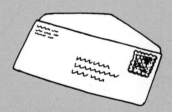

2. This is an envelope.

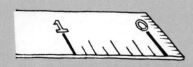

3. This is an inch.

4. This is an airplane.

Note: Use the definite article *the* with specific or particular nouns, either singular or plural.

5. This is an umbrella.

6. This is an earring.

7. This is an orange.

8. This is an egg.

9. This is an arm.

10. This is an eye.

11. This is an ear.

12. This is an elephant.

EXERCISES

A. Fill in the blanks with *a* or *an*.

1. This is ___*an*___ airplane.

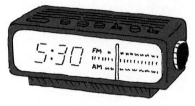

2. This is ___*a*___ radio.

3. This is _____ earring.

4. This is _____ orange.

5. This is _____ pear.

6. This is _____ elephant.

7. This is _____ ear.

8. This is _____ arm.

9. This is _____ egg.

10. This is _____ TV.

11. This is _____ desk.

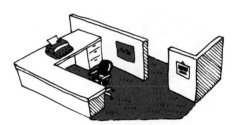

12. This is _____ office.

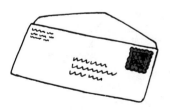

13. This is _____ envelope.

14. This is _____ umbrella.

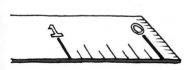

15. This is _____ inch.

16. This is _____ computer.

B. Fill in the blanks with *a* or *an* and the name of the object.

1. This is _____*a table*_____ .

2. This is _____*an earring*_____ .

3. This is _____ .

4. This is _____ .

5. This is _____ .

6. This is _____ .

7. This is _____ .

8. This is _____ .

9. This is _____ .

10. This is _____ .

11. This is _____ .

12. This is _____ .

C. Substitute the words in the sentence.

Example: This is a book.   eye
    This is an eye.
    This is a house.   house

1. chair	5. earring	9. inch	13. shoe
2. arm	6. TV	10. office	14. elephant
3. ear	7. egg	11. school	15. radio
4. orange	8. envelope	12. apple	16. umbrella

NEW WORDS

airplane	arm	egg	eye	orange
an	ear	elephant	inch	pear
apple	earring	envelope	office	umbrella

4 PLURAL OF NOUNS

Form the plural of nouns in the following ways:

1. Add *-s* to most nouns.

| one book | two books | one calculator | two calculators |

2. Add *-es* to most nouns that end in *-s, -sh, -ch,* or *-x.* Pronounce *-es* as a separate syllable.

| one box | two boxes | one bus | two buses |

3. Some nouns end in a consonant followed by *y.* They usually form the plural by dropping the *y* and adding *-ies.*

| one fly | two flies | one dictionary | two dictionaries |

4. Some nouns have special plural forms.

| one tooth | two teeth | one foot | two feet |

1. What's this?
   It's a lamp.

2. What are these?*
   They're lamps.

*The plural of *this* is *these. They're* is the contraction of *they are.*

18

3. What's this?
   It's a glass.

4. What are these?
   They're glasses.

5. What's this?
   It's a button.

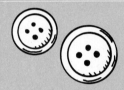

6. What are these?
   They're buttons.

7. What's this?
   It's a watch.

8. What are these?
   They're watches.

9. What's this?
   It's a bird.

10. What are these?
    They're birds.

EXERCISES

A. Answer the questions in complete sentences.

1. What are these?
   They're boxes.

2. What are these?
   They're buttons.

3. What are these?

4. What are these?

5. What are these?

6. What are these?

7. What are these?

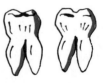

8. What are these?

9. What are these?

10. What are these?

11. What are these?

12. What are these?

13. What are these?

14. What are these?

15. What are these?

16. What are these?

B. Answer the questions in complete sentences.

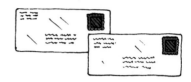

1. Are these boxes or envelopes?
   They're envelopes.

2. Are these shoes or boots?

3. Is this a chair or a table?

4. Are these buses or airplanes?

5. Are these ears or earrings?

6. Is this a radio or a television?

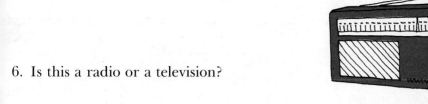

7. Is this a bird or a fly?

8. Is this a house or a school?

9. Are these glasses or buttons?

10. Are these oranges or apples?

New Words

are	button	glass	they
bird	calculator	lamp	they're
book	dictionary	one	tooth
box	fly	television	two
bus	foot	these	watch

5 DEMONSTRATIVE PRONOUNS:
Singular and Plural

This (singular) and *these* (plural) point out something near.
That (singular) and *those* (plural) point out something at a distance.
That's is the contraction of *that is*.

1. This is a door.
   That's a window.

2. This is a refrigerator.
   That's a stove.

3. This is a car.
   That's a boat.

4. This is a stamp.
   That's an envelope.

5. This is a letter.
   That's a mailbox.

6. These are doors.
   Those are windows.

7. These are refrigerators.
   Those are stoves.

8. These are cars.
   Those are boats.

9. These are stamps.
   Those are envelopes.

10. These are letters.
    Those are mailboxes.

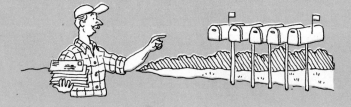

EXERCISES

A. Make the sentences plural.

1. This is a horse.
   These are horses.

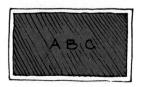

2. That's a blackboard.
   Those are blackboards.

3. That's a letter.

4. This is a stamp.

5. This is a boat.

6. That's a refrigerator.

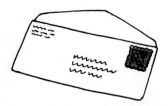

7. That's an envelope.

8. That's a bird.

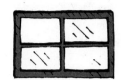

9. This is a window.

10. That's a fly.

1. This is a door.

12. That's a car.

3. That's an umbrella.

14. This is a flower.

5. This is a mailbox.

16. That's an island.

B. Fill in the blanks using *Is this* or *Are these* to complete the questions ar *It's* or *They're* to complete the answers.

1. ____*Is this*____ an apple or a pear?
   ____*It's*____ a pear.

2. _____ a desk or a blackboard?
   _____ a blackboard.

3. _____ dogs or horses?
   _____ horses.

4. _____ a boat or a car?
   _____ a car.

5. _____ dresses or coats?
   _____ dresses.

C. Fill in the blanks using *Is that* or *Are those* to complete the questions and *It's* or *They're* to complete the answers.

1. ___Is that___ a skirt or a pair of pants?
   ___It's___ a skirt.

2. _____ calculators or computers?
   _____ calculators.

3. _____ an elephant or a horse?
   _____ an elephant.

4. _____ a bird or an airplane?
   _____ an airplane.

NEW WORDS

blackboard	door	mailbox	that
boat	horse	refrigerator	that's
calculator	island	stamp	those
car	letter	stove	window

6 DESCRIPTIVE ADJECTIVES

A descriptive adjective modifies or describes a noun and usually precedes it.

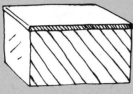

a big box

a little box

It has the same form before singular and plural nouns.

an old car

two old cars

It can also follow the verb *to be*.

The car is new.

The cars are new.

1. This is a tall person.*

2. This is a short person.

*The plural of *person* is *people*.

3. This is a full glass.

4. This is an empty glass.

5. That's a white cat.

6. That's a black cat.

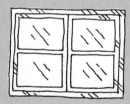

7. This is an open window.

8. This is a closed window.

9. This is a wet umbrella.

10. This is a dry umbrella.

EXERCISES

A. Fill in the blank with the adjective that best describes the picture.

1. These are ____*full*____ glasses.

2. That's an _____ shirt.

3. This is a _____ umbrella.

4. This is a _____ car.

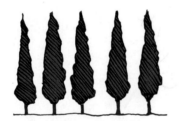

5. Those are _____ trees.

6. That's an _____ glass.

7. This is a _____ dog.

8. Those are _____ socks.

B. Make sentences with the following phrases.

1. that long skirt
   That skirt is long.

2. the white flowers
   The flowers are white.

3. the closed envelope

4. the big TV

5. this little fly

6. that wet person

NEW WORDS

big	empty	new	person
black	full	old	short
closed	little	open	tall
dry	long	people	wet
			white

7 SUBJECT PRONOUNS; SIMPLE PRESENT TENSE: *to be—Affirmative*

SUBJECT PRONOUNS

	Singular	*Plural*
1st person	I	we
2nd person	you	you
3rd person	he she it	they

It refers to a thing or an animal, but never a person.* *They* refers to things, animals, or people.

TO BE

	FULL FORMS		CONTRACTED FORMS	
	Singular	*Plural*	*Singular*	*Plural*
1st person	I am	we are	I'm	we're
2nd person	you are	you are	you're	you're
3rd person	he she is it	they are	he's she's it's	they're

When used with subject pronouns, the verb forms are usually shortened.

1. I'm a student.

2. Jim and I are students.

He and *she* are usually used with animals that are pets.

3. You're an accountant.

4. You and Ellen are accountants.

5. The man is a mechanic.

6. The women are mechanics.*

7. The woman is a doctor.

8. The men are doctors.*

9. The book is heavy.
It's a heavy book.

10. The books are heavy.
They're heavy books.

The plural forms of *man* and *woman* are irregular: *men, women.*

EXERCISES

A. Fill in the blanks with the correct form of the verb *to be*. Then, wherever possible, say each sentence, using the contracted form.

1. I _____*am*_____ a teacher.
   I'm a teacher.

2. Jill and I _____*are*_____ doctors.

3. They _____ mechanics.

4. He _____ a doctor.

5. They _____ heavy boxes.

6. Tom and Paula _____ students.

7. It _____ a black cat.

8. We _____ teachers.

9. You and Joe _____ accountants.

10. She _____ a mechanic.

1. They _____ empty glasses.

12. I _____ a student.

Substitute the words in the sentence. Use contractions when possible.

Example: I'm a doctor.   you (singular)
          You're a doctor.   they
          They're doctors.

you (plural)
they
we
I
she

6. Joe
7. he
8. Ana
9. Ana and Jack
10. they

11. she
12. you and Mike
13. Ellen and I
14. Al and Anita
15. Roy

1. Are the doors open or closed?
   They're closed.

2. Are you a doctor or an accountant?

3. Is the woman tall or short?

4. Are Jean and John students or
   accountants?

5. Is the person a man or a woman?

6. Is she a doctor or a mechanic?

7. Are the cars new or old?

8. Are they birds or cats?

9. Is this a glass or an envelope?

NEW WORDS

accountant	heavy	mechanic	we're
am	he's	she	woman
and	I	she's	you
doctor	I'm	teacher	you're
he	man	we	

8 SIMPLE PRESENT TENSE:
to be—Negative

Form the negative of *to be* by placing *not* after the verb.

FULL FORMS

I	am not	we are not
you	are not	you are not
he		
she	is not	they are not
it		

Contracted forms are commonly used. There are two contracted forms.

CONTRACTED FORMS

I'm	not	we're not	I'm	not	we aren't
you're	not	you're not	you	aren't	you aren't
he's			he		
she's	not	they're not	she	isn't	they aren't
it's			it		

1. I'm not hungry.
   I'm thirsty.

2. We're not thirsty.
   We're hungry.

40

3. You're not a teacher.
   You're a student.

4. You're not doctors.
   You're lawyers.

5. She's not a good student.
   She's a bad student.

6. They're not clean socks.
   They're dirty socks.

7. He's not an old teacher.
   He's a young teacher.

8. They're not short women.
   They're tall women.

9. It's not a cold iron.
   It's a hot iron.

10. They're not small rabbits.
    They're big rabbits.

EXERCISES

A. Substitute the words in the sentence. Use two contracted forms for each substitution when possible.

Example: I'm not a lawyer.

He's not a lawyer. He isn't a lawyer.
The men aren't lawyers.

he
the men

1. you (plural)
2. Susan
3. he
4. she
5. the woman

6. the man
7. they
8. we
9. she
10. I

11. the women
12. you (singular)
13. Jack and I
14. Ellen and Tom
15. Christine

B. Change the sentences to a contracted form of the negative.

1. Linda's a good student.
   Linda's not a good student. or
   Linda isn't a good student.

2. We're hot.
   We're not hot. or
   We aren't hot.

3. He's an accountant.

4. It's a young horse.

5. Victor is hungry.

6. She's thirsty.

7. He's a lawyer.

8. They're dirty boots.

9. That's a small house.

10. It's a clean blackboard.

11. You're a teacher.

12. I'm a mechanic.

C. Answer the questions. First give a negative answer, and then an affirmative answer. Use contracted forms in both.

1. Are Joe and Helen doctors?
No, Joe and Helen aren't doctors.
They're lawyers.

2. Is this an iron?
No, it's not (or it isn't) an iron.
It's a lamp.

3. Are you a teacher?

4. Are you a mechanic?

5. Are they rabbits?

6. Is Jack old?

7. Are you and Lee bad students?

8. Am I cold?

9. Is that a big rabbit?

10. Are Judy and Marie tall?

11. Is that a calculator?

12. Is the umbrella open?

13. Are the shoes clean?

14. Is the box empty?

NEW WORDS

aren't	dirty	iron	thirsty
bad	good	lawyer	young
clean	hot	rabbit	
cold	hungry	small	

9 SIMPLE PRESENT TENSE:
to be—Questions

Form questions with *to be* by placing the verb before the subject. Add a question mark at the end of the question.

Am I . . . . ?   Are we . . . . . ?
Are you. . . . . ?   Are you. . . . . ?
Is { he . . . . . . ?
she . . . . . ?   Are they . . . . ?
it . . . . ?

1. **Am I a good accountant?**
    Yes, you're a good accountant.

2. **Are you a typist?**
    Yes, I'm a typist.

3. **Is Ms. Lane a student?**
    Yes, she's a student.

4. **Is Steve a bad student?**
    Yes, he's a bad student.

5. **Is Mrs. Riva an artist?**
    Yes, she's an artist.

6. **Is he a mail carrier?**
    Yes, he's a mail carrier.

7. Is this a chicken?
   Yes, it's a chicken.

8. Are we late?
   Yes, you're late.

9. Are you dentists?
   Yes, we're dentists.

10. Are Laura and Bill police officers?
    Yes, they're police officers.

11. Are they musicians?
    Yes, they're musicians.

12. Are Barbara and Joy doctors?
    Yes, they're doctors.

13. Are they good dancers?
    Yes, they're good dancers.

14. Are these bananas?
    Yes, they're bananas.

EXERCISES

A. Substitute the subject in each question.

Example: Am *I* a good typist?   Don and Peggy
Are Don and Peggy good typists?

1. you (plural)
2. you and I
3. we
4. Mrs. Thomas

5. he
6. George and Joe
7. they
8. you (singular)

9. Barbara
10. she
11. Betty and I
12. I

B. Change the sentences to questions.

1. Mr. Ross is a word processor.
   Is Mr. Ross a word processor?

2. We're good typists.
   Are we good typists?

3. You're a computer programmer.

4. They're artists.

5. The glass is empty.

6. That man is a nurse.

7. The woman is a police officer.

8. This is a banana.

9. He's a waiter.

10. I'm late.

11. Ms. Lopez is a dancer.

12. The chicken is big.

13. The window is open.

14. The umbrellas are wet.

C. Answer the questions in complete sentences.

1. Are you an artist or a dancer?

2. Is Miss Pace a musician or a dentist?

3. Are these chickens or rabbits?

4. Are Dr. James and I doctors or dentists?

5. Is this a pear or a banana?

6. Is that a fish or a bird?

7. Are they word processors or
   mail carriers?

8. Is this a VCR or a computer?

9. Are these glasses or pencils?

0. Are elephants big or little?

NEW WORDS

artist	dentist	Miss	nurse
banana	Dr.	Mr.	police officer
chicken	fish	Mrs.	typist
computer programmer	late	Ms.	VCR
dancer	mail carrier	musician	waiter
			word processor

10 QUESTIONS WITH *WHERE*; PREPOSITIONS

Where is a question word. It asks about location. The contraction of *where is* is *where's*. *Where are* is not contracted.

> *Where is the computer?*   or   *Where's the computer?*
> *Where are the computers?*

The answer to a *where* question often includes a prepositional phrase that indicates place.

The computer is *on the desk.*

1. Where's the lamp?
   It's on the desk.

2. Where are the keys?
   They're in the drawer.

3. Where's the cat?
   It's under the sofa.

4. Where's the suitcase?
   It's above the seat.

5. Where's the little girl?
   She's at school.

6. Where's the big boy?
   He's at home.

7. Where are the children?*
   They're in the park.

8. Where are the apples?
   They're in the bowl.

9. Where's Walt?
   He's behind Susan.

10. Where's Susan?
    She's in front of Walt.

11. Where's the television set?
    It's between the lamp and
    the chair.

12. Where's the typewriter?
    It's between the books and the
    lamp.

*The singular of *children* is *child*.

EXERCISES

A.   Fill in the blanks with the correct preposition.

1.   The picture is _____*on*_____ the wall.

2.   The computer is _____ the box.

3.   The children are _____ home.

4.   Mary is _____ Bill.

5.   The dog is _____ the chair.

6.   The picture is _____ the chair.

7.   The television is _____ the sofa.

8.   The cat is _____ the boy and the girl.

B. Here are some answers. Write a *where* question for each one.

1. The keys are on the book.
   Where are the keys?

2. The cat is in the suitcase.
   Where's the cat?

3. The airplane is above the park.

4. Alice is in front of the house.

5. The door is between the window
   and the television.

6. The children are at school.

7. He's behind the sofa.

8. The mechanic is under the car.

C. Ask about the location of each person or thing listed below. Then answer your question.

1. man
   Where's the man?
   He's at the office.

2. typist

3. fly

4. stamp

5. letter

D. Draw the objects and the person in the places named in the instructions.

1. a glass on the table
2. flowers in the glass
3. a picture above the chair
4. a lamp on the table
5. a pair of boots under the table

6. a book between the glass and the lamp
7. a cat behind the chair
8. a person in the chair

NEW WORDS

above	child	in	seat	wall
behind	drawer	key	sofa	where
between	front (in front of)	on	suitcase	where's
bowl	girl	park	typewriter	
boy	home	picture	under	

11 THERE IS, THERE ARE: SOME, ANY

There + *is* or *are* shows that something exists in a particular place. *There is (there's)* is used with singular nouns. *There are* is used with plural nouns.

There's a book on the table.

There are five flowers in the vase.

In questions, *is* or *are* comes before *there*.

> *Is there a book on the table?*
> *Are there five flowers in the vase?*

The negative singular answer can appear two ways.

> *No, there isn't a book on the table.*
> *No, there's no book on the table.*

When no numbers are given in plural questions and answers, *any* is usually used in questions, *some* in affirmative answers, and *any* in negative answers.

Are there any flowers in the vase?
No, there aren't any flowers in the vase.

Are there any plants on the floor?
Yes, there are some plants on the floor.

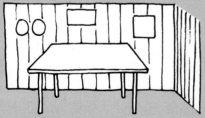

1. There's a table in the dining room.

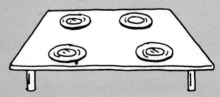

2. There are four plates on the table.

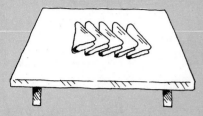

3. There are some napkins on the table.

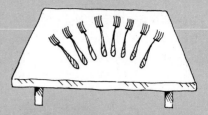

4. There are some forks on the table.

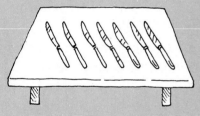

5. There are some knives* on the table.

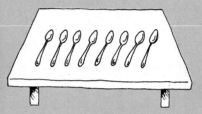

6. There are some spoons on the table.

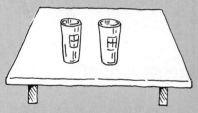

7. There are two glasses on the table.

8. There are three bowls of vegetables on the table.

9. There's a salt shaker on the table.

10. There's a pepper shaker on the table.

*The singular of *knives* is *knife*.

EXERCISES

A. **Substitute the words in the sentence.**

Example: There's a chair in the room.
        There are some cats in the room.
        There are three chairs in the room.

        some cats
        three chairs

1. a television
2. two tables
3. three pictures
4. a window

5. some lamps
6. a sofa
7. some bowls
8. a bird

9. two dogs
10. a fish
11. a radio
12. a dictionary

B. **Change each sentence first to a question and then to a negative answer. Use the contracted forms *there's*, *there's no*, and *there aren't any*.**

1. There's a salt shaker on the table.
    Is there a salt shaker on the table?
    No, there's no salt shaker on the table.

2. There are some chairs in the kitchen.
    Are there any chairs in the kitchen?
    No, there aren't any chairs in the kitchen.

3. There are some children in the park.

4. There are some plates on the table.

5. There are some vegetables in the bowl.

6. There's a fork on the plate.

7. There are some napkins on the table.

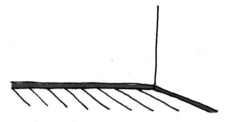

8. There are some pictures on the wall.

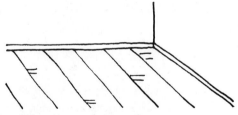

9. There are some plants on the floor.

10. There are some flowers in the vase.

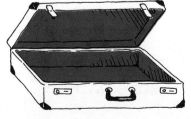

11. There's a shirt in the suitcase.

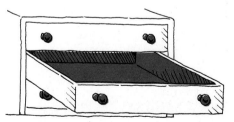

12. There are some stamps in the drawer.

C. Answer the questions in complete sentences. Use contractions when possible.

1. Is there a spoon or a fork on this plate?
   There's a fork on this plate.

2. Is there an apple or a banana in this bowl?

3. Are there plates or glasses on this table?

4. Is there a salt shaker or a pepper shaker on this table?

. Are there napkins or flowers on this table?

Is there a table or a chair in this kitchen?

Are there cats or dogs under this table?

NEW WORDS

dining room	four	pepper shaker	spoon
five	kitchen	plant	three
floor	knife	plate	vase
fork	napkin	salt shaker	vegetable

12 SIMPLE PRESENT TENSE:
Affirmative

The simple present tense describes an action which occurs regularly or usually.

Jack likes apples. (generally)

It often appears with a phrase that tells time or frequency.

Jack often walks to school.
He often walks to school in the morning.

To WALK

I	walk	we walk
you	walk	you walk
he		
she	walks	they walk
it		

All forms of the simple present tense are the same except for the third person singular. Add *-s* to the third person singular ending in a consonant *(walk, eat)* or in *-e (take).*

He drinks coffee every morning.
She likes vanilla ice cream.

Add *-es* to verbs ending in any other vowel *(a, i, o, u)* or to some verbs ending in three consonants.

Kathy goes to work every day.
Rich does some homework every evening.
Sally watches television every night.

1. You eat breakfast every morning.

2. I walk to school every morning.

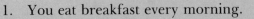

. He takes a bus to the office every day.

4. She usually takes a subway to the office.

. We often walk to work.

6. You and Rosa always walk to school.

. They always take a train to the city.

8. Ray goes to work every day.

I have a new car.

10. He has an old car.

EXERCISES

A. Substitute the subject in the sentence.

Example: I usually walk to the store.   he
He usually walks to the store.

1. you
2. you and Peggy
3. she
4. we

5. he
6. they
7. Andy and Rich
8. that girl

9. Jenny and
10. Fran
11. I
12. the childre:

B. Substitute the subjects listed in exercise A in this sentence.

Example: I always drink coffee in the morning.   he
He always drinks coffee in the morning.

C. Substitute the subjects listed in exercise A in this sentence.

Example: I go to the city every day.   he
He goes to the city every day.

D. Substitute the subjects listed in exercise A in this sentence.

Example: I have some keys.   he
He has some keys.

E. Fill in the blanks with the correct form of the verb in parentheses.

. I ___*walk*___ home every day.
(walk)

. Leland always _____ to restaurants. (go)

. Tom usually _____ the mail on the desk. (put)

. She _____ the newspaper every day. ((read)

. I often _____ to the movies. (go)

6. I _____ homework every evening. (do)

7. Ann always _____ taxis. (take)

8. We _____ a bus to school in the morning. (take)

9. Richard and I _____ in New York. (live)

10. Bob usually _____ breakfast. (eat)

1. Carol _____ television every evening. (watch)

2. They _____ animals. (like)

3. You always _____ good books. (read)

4. They _____ letters every evening. (write)

NEW WORDS

always	eat	mail	subway
animal	evening	morning	take
breakfast	every	movies	taxi
city	go	night	train
coffee	have	often	usually
day	homework	put	vanilla
do	ice cream	read	walk (v)
drink (v)	like (v)	restaurant	watch (v)
drive (v)	live (v)	store	work
			write (v)

13 SIMPLE PRESENT TENSE:
Negative

The negative of the simple present tense places *do not* or *does not* in front of the verb.

FULL FORMS		CONTRACTED FORMS	
I do not walk	we do not walk	I don't walk	we don't
you do not walk	you do not walk	you don't walk	you don't
he she it } does not walk	they do not walk	he she it } doesn't walk	they don't

1. I don't walk to school.
   I run.

2. You don't take the bus to work.
   You drive.

3. Dick doesn't go to the movies often.
   He prefers the theater.

4. Laura doesn't work in an office.
   She works in a factory.

5. The cat doesn't like dogs.
   It likes mice.*

6. Nick and I usually don't travel by train.
   We travel by plane.

7. You and Maggie don't eat lunch at one
   o'clock.
   You both eat lunch at noon.

8. Norma and David usually don't eat
   dinner at home.
   They eat in a restaurant.

The singular of *mice* is *mouse*.

EXERCISES

A. Substitute the subject of the sentence.

Example: We don't live in New York. George
George doesn't live in New York.

1. Joan and I
2. Pete
3. Lee and Amy
4. you

5. I
6. Barbara
7. you two
8. Mrs. Faro

9. they
10. you and Sid
11. we
12. she

B. Change the sentences to the negative. Use contractions.

1. I go to work by car.
I don't go to work by car.

2. We walk to work.

3. You like the movies.

4. You two go to the factory every day.

5. Lee eats lunch at two o'clock.

6. They often go to the theater.

7. Barbara works in the evening.

8. We like to travel by plane.

9. Mr. and Mrs. Crane work in a restaurant.

10. I eat breakfast in the morning.

C. Give an affirmative answer and then a negative answer to each question.

1. Do you go to work by bus or by train?
   I go to work by train.
   I don't go to work by bus.

2. Does Pete take the bus to work or does he walk?

3. Do you both usually go to the movies or to the theater?

4. Do they travel by train or by plane?

5. Do these people like chocolate or vanilla ice cream?

6. Does she like pears or oranges?

7. Do you have lunch at home or in a restaurant?

8. Does he put the mail on the desk or in the drawer?

9. Do Liz and Gary have a new suitcase or an old suitcase?

10. Do the students go to school by subway or by bus?

11. Does the child prefer cats or mice?

12. Does she eat lunch at one or two o'clock?

13. Does he read a newspaper or a book in the morning?

14. Do the children have bicycles or cars?

New Words

bicycle	factory	plane
both	lunch	prefer
by	mouse	run (v)
chocolate	noon	theater
dinner	o'clock	travel (v)

14 SIMPLE PRESENT TENSE: *Questions*

Simple present tense questions place the auxiliary *do* or *does* before the subject. Except for the verb *to be*, almost all verbs use *do* in simple present questions. *Do* has no meaning in these questions.*

Do	I	speak English?	Do we	speak English?
Do	you	speak English?	Do you	speak English?
Does	he / she / it	speak English?	Do they	speak English?

Answer these questions with a short answer and *do* or *does,* or a long answer.

Question: *Do you like animals?*

Answers: **Affirmative**
            Yes, I do.   or
            Yes, I like animals.

            Negative
            No, I don't.   or
            No, I don't like animals.

1. **Do you know Charles?**
    Yes, I do.

2. **Does Lisa have a VCR?**
    Yes, she does.

*See the note on page 93.

3. Do we speak English at school?
Yes, you do.

4. Does the store sell fresh vegetables?
No, it doesn't.

5. Do you drink milk?
No, I don't.

6. Do you eat eggs?
Yes, I do.

7. Do the children want any cookies?
Yes, they do.

8. Does Big Joe like meat?
No, he doesn't.

9. Do you and Ronnie eat fish?
Yes, we do.

10. Do they cook at home?
Yes, they do.

EXERCISES

A. **Substitute the subject of this question.**

Example: Do you watch television every evening?   I
Do I watch television every evening?

1. the girl
2. Elaine
3. Helen and Jenny
4. Linda

5. they
6. he
7. Rob and I
8. we

9. she
10. you
11. Mr. and Mrs. Green
12. you and David

B. **Change the statements to questions. Then answer each question using a short answer with *do* or *does*.**

1. She goes to school.
   Does she go to school?
   Yes, she does.

2. They live in this house.

3. Joe has a new shirt.

4. Sue knows Lee.

5. They have a big dinner every evening.

6. He speaks English.

7. Carol takes a bus to work.

8. They eat breakfast.

9. She likes milk.

10. We have a VCR.

C. Answer the questions in complete sentences. Use contractions when possible.

1. Do you and Jane like animals?
   No, we don't like animals.

2. Do they speak English at home?

3. Is she in school now?

4. Do you eat lunch at noon?

5. Does Helen have a new car?

6. Do they want any cookies?

New Words

cook (v)	know (v)	sell (v)
cookie	meat	speak (v)
drink (v)	milk	want (v)
fresh		

15 REVIEW

A. Change the verbs from singular to plural and make any necessary changes.

1. Does he speak English?
   Do they speak English?

2. This is a computer.

3. The man doesn't work in this school.

4. That's a fly.

5. It's a black horse.

6. Does the child eat ice cream every evening.

7. Is there an apple in the bowl?

8. The accountant doesn't eat in that restaurant.

9. Is the knife in the drawer?

10. I'm not thirsty.

B. Change the statements to questions and answer in the negative.

1. We put the plate between the knife and the spoon.
   Do you put the plate between the knife and the spoon?
   No, we don't put the plate between the knife and the spoon.

2. This is a full plate.

3. They sell fresh meat in that store.

4. She has two new suitcases.

5. There's some chocolate in these cookies.

6. We have some stamps.

7. The umbrella is wet.

8. Those mechanics usually work in the morning.

C. Answer the questions in complete sentences.

1. Where's the computer programmer?
She's between the artist and the dancer.

2. Where are the children?

3. What's this?

4. Where's the dress?

5. Does the woman take the train to work?

6. Is the man in front of the chair?

7. Where are the birds?

8. Is the computer between the lamp and the VCR?

16 OBJECT PRONOUNS

Use the object pronoun form for the object of a preposition or the direct or indirect object of a verb.

	SINGULAR			PLURAL	
Subject		*Object*		*Subject*	*Object*
I		me		we	us
you		you		you	you
he		him			
she		her		they	them
it		it			

Some verbs can be followed by both an indirect and a direct object. When the direct object is a noun, the indirect object can precede or follow the noun.

> *He sends you a letter every week.* (preposition not included)
> *He sends a letter to you every week.* (preposition included)

If the direct object is a pronoun, the indirect object and its preposition must follow.

> *He sends it to you every week.*

1. I always walk to school with Mother.
   I always walk to school with her.
   She always walks to school with me.

2. Phil and I see Andrea every morning.
   We see her every morning.
   She sees us every morning.

82

3. I teach English to the students.
       I teach English to them.
       I teach them English.
       I teach it to them.

4. Vanna sells dresses to Beatrice and me.
       She sells dresses to us.
       She sells us dresses.
       She sells them to us.

5. We send postcards to Father.
       We send postcards to him.
       We send him postcards.
       We send them to him.

6. You and Al buy toys for the little girl.
       You buy toys for her.
       You buy her toys.
       You buy them for her.

7. They give the money to Victor and
Lisa.
       They give the money to them.
       They give them the money.
       They give it to them.

EXERCISES

A. Substitute the correct object pronoun or pronouns for the words in italics.

1. He sells *books* to *John.*
   He sells them to him.

2. She gives meat *to the dog.*

3. We often see *Mr. and Mrs. Lopez.*

4. They study English with *Mother and me.*

5. I know *Vanna.*

6. Father usually buys toys *for the children.*

7. Roberto has dinner with *Alicia and me.*

8. He always eats with *you and Lucy.*

B. Choose the correct form.

1. (*We,* Us) work with (*them,* they) at the factory.

2. (Me, I) know (she, her) and Barry.

3. (They, Them) often buy toys for (he, him).

4. (Him, He) and (I, me) always eat dinner at home.

5. (We, Us) give (him, he) the money every week.

6. (Her, She) and (me, I) buy (he, him) food every day.

7. (He, Him) sells (I, me) flowers every day.

8. (Us, We) teach English to (they, them).

C. Substitute the correct subject and object pronouns for the words in italics.

1. *Mrs. Herman* sells *eggs* to *Sue and me*.
   She sells them to us.

2. *Jack and I* write *Mother* postcards every
   week.

3. *Sally and Fred* send *the children* to camp.

4. *You and Alice* often buy *flowers* from the
   florist.

NEW WORDS

buy	give	money	teach
camp	her	mother	them
father	him	postcard	toy
florist	me	see	us
food		send	week
			with

85

17 POSSESSIVE ADJECTIVES; POSSESSIVE PRONOUNS

The possessive adjective comes before the noun it modifies and agrees in gender and number with the possessor, not the noun.

> *I have my key.*
> *I have their key.*

> *I have my keys.*
> *I have their keys.*

Use a possessive pronoun to avoid repeating the noun.

> *This is my key.*
> *These keys are my keys.*

> *This key is mine.*
> *These keys are mine.*

	SINGULAR			**PLURAL**	
Subject	*Possessive Adjective*	*Possessive Pronoun*	*Subject*	*Possessive Adjective*	*Possessive Pronoun*
I	my	mine	we	our	ours
you	your	yours	you	your	yours
he	his	his			
she	her	hers	they	their	theirs
it	its	its			

1. This is my raincoat.
    That's your raincoat.

2. Mine is long.
    Yours is short.

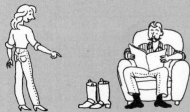 

3. Those are his boots.

4. His have buckles.

5. Those are her boots.

6. Hers have zippers.

7. Where are our hats?

8. Here they are. These are ours.

9. Where are your disks?

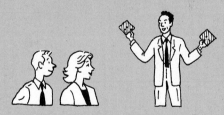

10. Here they are. These are yours.

11. I see their barbecue.

12. Theirs is electric.

EXERCISES

A. Change the words in italics to a new subject and a corresponding possessive adjective.

Example: *I do my homework every evening.*   you
             You do your homework every evening.

1. you and I	4. Alex and Ted	7. she
2. he	5. they	8. you and Brian
3. Carol	6. we	9. the children

B. Using the example and items in exercise A, make new sentences replacing *my homework* with the appropriate forms of the possessive pronoun.

Example: *I do mine every evening.*   you
             You do yours every evening.

C. Give an affirmative and then a negative answer to each question.

1. Is that her disk or yours?
It's her disk.
It isn't mine.

2. Is that your money or his?

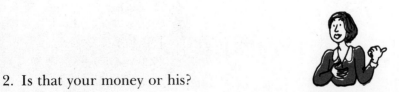

3. Are those their raincoats or ours?

2. Is this my sandwich or yours?

. Are these our postcards or yours?

. Are those his boots or hers?

. Is that his milkshake or hers?

8. Is this her hat or mine?

9. Are those your bicycles or theirs?

10. Is this her dish or ours?

11. Are these their socks or ours?

12. Is that our barbecue or theirs?

C. Replace the forms of *to belong* in each sentence with the correct forms of *to be*. Then substitute the correct possessive pronoun for each object pronoun or noun.

1. The black book belongs to me.
   The black book is mine.

2. That barbecue belongs to us.

3. Those plants belong to them.

4. The lamp belongs to you.

5. The flowers belong to her.

6. This money belongs to you.

7. That raincoat belongs to Mr. Smith.*

8. Those shoes belong to that girl.

9. That dress belongs to Patricia.

10. This car belongs to us.

NEW WORDS

barbecue	electric	mine	sandwich
belong to	hat	my	their
buckle	his	our	theirs
dish	its	ours	your
disk	milkshake	raincoat	yours
			zipper

To form the possessive of singular nouns, including proper names, add *'s*.
That hat is Mr. Smith's. Those are Ross's boots. This is the teacher's coat.
To form the possessive of plural nouns, add *'s*.
Those are the teachers' raincoats.

18 YES/NO QUESTIONS AND SHORT ANSWERS; INFORMATION QUESTIONS

Simple questions are formed by reversing the subject and the verb in the 9 statement. Simple questions are answered with *yes* or *no* plus either a complete answer or a short answer.

Are you happy?

Complete answer:	Yes, I'm happy.	No, I'm not happy.
Short answer:	Yes, I am.	No, I'm not.

Do you speak English?

Complete answer:	Yes, I speak English.	No, I don't speak English
Short answer:	Yes, I do.	No, I don't.

Information questions usually require a complete answer. They begin with one of the question words: *who, what, where, when, why,* or *how.*

1. Use *who* to ask about people.

Who's at the door?
It's your grandfather.

Who's in the living room?
Your grandmother's there.

2. Use *what* to ask about a person's job.

What do you do?*
I'm an electrician.

What is he?
He's a plumber.

*In this sense, *do* is used idiomatically to ask about a person's profession.
What does Jean do? She's a doctor.

Use *what* to introduce general questions.

What do you eat for breakfast?
I eat toast with butter.

What's your name?
My name is Rita Gomez.

Use *where* to ask about location.

Where's the post office?
It's on Main Street.

Where does he live?
He lives in Los Angeles.

Use *when* to ask about time.

When does the play begin?
It begins at eight o'clock.

When's your class?
It's at nine o'clock.

Use *how* to ask about manner and quality.

How are you?
I'm fine, thank you.

How does he feel today?
He feels fine.

EXERCISES

A. Answer the questions using an affirmative short answer and then a negative short answer.

1. Is he hungry?
    Yes, he is.
    No, he isn't.   or   *No, he's not.*

2. Are the suitcases in the living room?

3. Is the window closed?

4. Do they like pears?

5. Does she have a dictionary?

6. Are Lee and Jan at the play?

7. Do you have any money?

8. Am I late?

9. Does this money belong to you?

10. Are you always home in the evening?

B. Starting with a question word, ask a question that corresponds to each answer.

1. The classes begin in the evening.
    When do the classes begin?

2. Mr. and Mrs. Chen live across the street.

3. Your grandfather is in the kitchen.

4. I'm fine, thank you.

. Elena is a lawyer.

6. He feels sad today.

. Shao Li is at the door.

8. I eat fish and vegetables for dinner.

NEW WORDS

across	electrician	happy	plumber	toast
begin	feel	how	post office	when
butter	fine	name	sad	who
class	grandfather	nine	street	
eight	grandmother	play	there	

19 PRESENT CONTINUOUS TENSE:
Affirmative

The present continuous tense describes an action which is occurring now. This tense uses the present forms of *to be* and the *-ing* form of the main verb.

FULL FORMS		CONTRACTED FORMS	
I am walking	we are walking	I'm walking	we're walking
you are walking	you are walking	you're walking	you're walking
he ⎫		he's ⎫	
she ⎬ is walking	they are walking	she's ⎬ walking	they're walking
it ⎭		it's ⎭	

1. I'm standing.

2. Now, I'm sitting.*

3. I'm closing the door now.**

4. Maria is doing her homework.

5. Phil and Beverly are studying algebra together.

6. It's snowing today.

*Some verbs ending in a vowel and a consonant double the final consonant before adding *-ing*: *put—putting, sit—sitting, run—running, get—getting,* and so on.

**Most verbs ending in a vowel + consonant + final *e* drop the final *e* before adding *-ing*: *close—closing, write—writing,* and so on.

7. We're reading magazines.

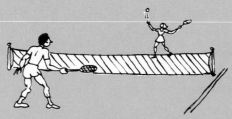

8. They're playing tennis.

9. Steve is putting the dishes in the dishwasher.

10. Sara is talking on the telephone.

11. The teacher is explaining the algebra lesson.

12. Her students are learning a lot.

13. My grandfather and grandmother are laughing.

14. The baby is crying.

EXERCISES

A. Substitute the subject of the sentence. Use contractions when possible.

Example: I'm studying English now.   you
               You're studying English now.

1. you and I
2. he
3. Akiyoshi
4. Akiyoshi and Ramon

5. they
6. she
7. she and I
8. you and Carla

9. we
10. you two
11. those people
12. the boys

B. Fill in the blanks with the present continuous form of the verb in parentheses. Use contractions when possible.

1. (You) ____*You've working*____ in a store now.   (work)

2. (Alicia) _____ to Sidney.   (talk)

3. (He) _____ the door.   (open)

4. (I) _____ a letter to my grandmother.   (write)

5. (You) _____ a book.   (read)

6. (It) _____ today.   (rain)

7. (They) _____ to work.   (walk)

8. (We) _____ to the movies.   (go)

9. (His grandfather) _____ the lesson to him.   (explain)

10. (Jackie and Daniela) _____ .   (laugh)

11. (She) _____ the dishes in the dishwasher.   (put)

12. (I) _____ my algebra homework.   (do)

C. Answer the questions in complete sentences.

1. Is Jay walking toward the door or toward the window?
He's walking toward the door.

2. Is Elena opening the box or the drawer?

3. Where's she going?

4. Are Diana and Barbara singing together?

5. Am I getting a book or a magazine?

6. Are you walking or running?

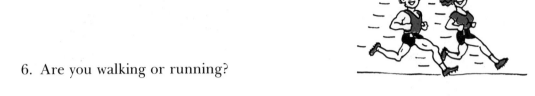

7. Are they traveling by bus or by plane?

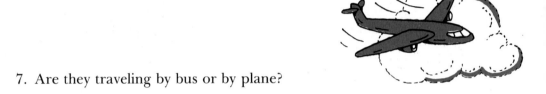

8. Are Willie and Ana playing baseball or tennis?

9. Are they laughing or crying?

10. Is he opening or closing the door?

1. Is the cat sleeping or running?

2. What's the dog doing?

3. Are you reading a magazine or writing a postcard?

4. Is she buying or selling the car?

New Words

a lot	dishwasher	lesson	sing	talk (v)
algebra	explain	magazine	sit	telephone
baseball	get	now	sleep (v)	tennis
close (v)	laugh (v)	open (v)	snow (v)	together
cry (v)	learn	play (v)	stand (v)	toward

20 PRESENT CONTINUOUS TENSE: *Negative*

To form the negative of the present continuous tense, place *not* after the present forms of *to be*. The negative of the present continuous tense has two contracted for[ms].

FULL FORMS

I am not walking	we are not walking
you are not walking	you are not walking
he she it is not walking	they are not walking

CONTRACTED FORMS

1

I'm not walking	we're not walking
you're not walking	you're not walking
he's she's it's not walking	they're not walking

2

I'm not walking	we aren't walking
you aren't walking	you aren't walking
he she it isn't walking	they aren't walking

1. I'm not studying geography now.
   I'm studying history.

2. You're not sitting at the desk.
   You're sitting at the table.

3. Jack isn't sitting down.
   He's standing up.

4. Linda isn't going down the stairs.
   She's going up the stairs.

5. It's not snowing today.
   It's raining.

6. We're not speaking English now.
   We're speaking Italian.

7. You and Ray aren't writing on
   the blackboard.
   You're writing in your
   notebooks.

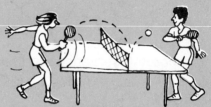

8. Gene and Lola aren't playing
   baseball.
   They're playing table tennis.

9. I'm not washing the floor.
   I'm washing the windows.

10. We're not working now.
    We're traveling.

1. They're not going to school.
   They're going to the library.

12. Beatrice and Jose aren't singing.
    They're dancing.

EXERCISES

A. Substitute the subject of the sentence. Use contracted forms when possible.

Example: I'm not washing the windows now.   she
She's not washing the windows now.   or *She isn't washing the windows now.*

1. you
2. he
3. your secretary
4. I

5. your mother and father
6. Mr. Roe and I
7. Mrs. Takashi
8. they

9. Ms. Stone
10. we
11. Jan
12. her grandmother

B. Change the sentences to the negative.

1. He's eating breakfast now.
He's not eating breakfast now. or *He isn't eating breakfast now.*

2. She's talking to the plumber.

3. They're sending money to their grandfather.

4. You're sitting in my chair.

5. I'm eating a sandwich for lunch.

6. We're putting our letters in the mailbox.

7. You and Paul are studying Italian.

8. He's eating his lunch now.

9. She's talking with the teacher.

10. They're sitting at the table.

11. I'm doing my homework.

12. We're playing table tennis.

C. Answer the questions. First give an affirmative answer and then a negative answer.

1. Are they sitting down or standing up?
   They're standing up.
   They're not sitting down.

2. Is she running or walking?

3. Is he sitting near the window or near the door?

4. Are you studying French or Spanish?

5. Is Pete studying or sleeping?

6. Is it raining or snowing?

NEW WORDS

dance (v)	geography	library	rain (v)	table tennis
down	history	near	Spanish	up
French	Italian	notebook	stairs	wash (v)

21 PRESENT CONTINUOUS TENSE: *Questions*

Form questions in the present continuous tense by placing the present form of *to be* before the subject.

Am	I walking?	Are we walking?
Are	you walking	Are you walking?
Is	he she walking? it	Are they walking?

1. Is that woman selling fruit?
   Yes, she's selling fruit.

2. Is Mr. Benson pointing to the strawberries?
   Yes, he's pointing to the strawberries.

3. Is he buying some strawberries?
   Yes, he's buying some strawberries.

4. Is the woman selling cherries too?
   Yes, she's selling cherries too.

5. What are the brothers asking for?
   They're asking for some cherries.

6. What are they forgetting?
   They're forgetting the cherries.

7. What's their sister doing?
   She's getting the cherries.

8. What are they doing now?
   They're eating the cherries.

EXERCISES

A. **Substitute the subject of the sentence.**

Example: Is she paying for the strawberries?   you
Are you paying for the strawberries?

1. I
2. they
3. we

4. the woman
5. he
6. the boys

7. she
8. Nina
9. Kathy and I

B. **Change the statements to questions.**

1. Jill is walking to work now.
   Is Jill walking to work now?

2. We're eating dinner.

3. It's snowing.

4. The children are playing in the park.

5. You and your sister are opening a new store.

6. They're studying Italian.

7. Maria is paying for some fruit.

8. She's giving the cookies to her brother.

9. Marcia is crying.

10. The children are sleeping.

C. Answer in complete sentences.

1. What's the man selling?
    He's selling fruit.

2. Who's pointing to the oranges?

3. What's the woman buying?

4. What else is the man selling?

5. What are the brothers asking for?

6. What are they eating?

NEW WORDS

ask for	forget
brother	fruit
cherry	sister
else	strawberry

22 NUMBERS: Cardinals and Ordinals

CARDINAL NUMBERS

These numbers are used for counting. They answer the question "How many?"

0 zero	10 ten	20 twenty
1 one	11 eleven	21 twenty-one
2 two	12 twelve	22 twenty-two
3 three	13 thirteen	23 twenty-three
4 four	14 fourteen	24 twenty-four
5 five	15 fifteen	25 twenty-five
6 six	16 sixteen	26 twenty-six
7 seven	17 seventeen	27 twenty-seven
8 eight	18 eighteen	28 twenty-eight
9 nine	19 nineteen	29 twenty-nine

30 thirty	101 one hundred one
31 thirty-one	102 one hundred two
40 forty	200 two hundred
41 forty-one	201 two hundred one
50 fifty	300 three hundred
60 sixty	400 four hundred
70 seventy	500 five hundred
80 eighty	1,000 one thousand
90 ninety	1,001 one thousand one
100 one hundred	2,000 two thousand

Addition

Two plus three $\left\{\begin{array}{c} \text{is} \\ \text{equals} \end{array}\right\}$ five. $2 + 3 = 5$

Five plus six is eleven. $5 + 6 = 11$

Subtraction

Seven minus four is three. $7 - 4 = 3$

Nine minus five is four. $9 - 5 = 4$

Multiplication

Two times eight is sixteen. $2 \times 8 = 16$

Four times seven is twenty-eight. $4 \times 7 = 28$

Division

Eight divided by four is two. $8 \div 4 = 2$

Twenty divided by two is ten. $20 \div 2 = 10$

ORDINAL NUMBERS

These are numbers like *first, second, third, fourth, fifth, sixth, seventh, eighth, ninth, tenth, eleventh, twelfth*. They describe position or order in a series.

This is my **first** English class. I live on **twelfth** street.

EXERCISES

A. Answer the questions in complete sentences.

1. How much is three plus four?
   Three plus four equals seven.

2. How much is six plus five?

3. How much is ten plus seven?

4. How much is eighteen plus ten?

5. How much is three times three?

6. How much is six times two?

7. How much is four times three?

8. How much is two times two?

9. How much is eight minus five?

10. How much is seven minus three?

11. How much is six minus two?

12. How much is ten minus five?

13. How much is eight divided by four?

14. How much is twelve divided by three?

15. How much is twenty-one divided by seven?

16. How much is eighty-one divided by nine?

B. Read these problems aloud and give the correct answers.

1. $4 + 2 =$	6. $10 - 4 =$	11. $12 - 2 =$
2. $9 - 6 =$	7. $20 \times 2 =$	12. $5 \times 3 =$
3. $3 \times 2 =$	8. $6 \div 3 =$	13. $73 + 41 =$
4. $10 \div 5 =$	9. $36 + 3 =$	14. $57 - 17 =$
5. $3 + 4 =$	10. $12 \div 4 =$	15. $63 \div 7 =$

NEW WORDS

add	fifth	ninety	subtract
addition	fifty	ninth	subtraction
divide	first	plus	ten
division	forty	second	tenth
eighteen	fourteen	seven	third
eighth	fourth	seventeen	thirteen
eighty	hundred	seventh	thirty
eleven	minus	seventy	thousand
eleventh	multiplication	six	times
equal	multiply	sixth	twelfth
fifteen	nineteen	sixty	twelve
			twenty

23

1. What time is it by this clock?
It's four o'clock.

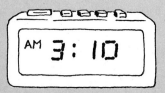

2. What time is it now?
It's ten after three.

3. What time is it now?
It's a quarter after three. or
It's three fifteen.

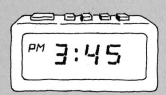

4. What time is now?
It's half past three. or
It's three thirty.

5. What time is it now?
It's twenty to four.

6. What time is it now?
It's a quarter to four.

7. What time is it?
It's 7 A.M.*

8. What time is it?
It's 10 P.M.**

*A.M. is the abbreviation for the Latin words, *ante meridiem.* This means "before noon" and indicates the moring hours from midnight to noon.

**P.M. is the abbreviation for the Latin words, *post meridiem.* This means "after noon" and indicates the afternoon and evening hours from noon to midnight.

9. Dollars are usually made of paper.

10. Cents are metal coins.

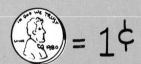 = 1¢

 = 5¢

11. A penny is worth one cent.

12. A nickel is worth five cents.

 = 10¢

= 25¢

13. A dime is worth ten cents.

14. A quarter is worth twenty-five cents.

= 50¢

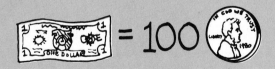 = 100

15. A half dollar is worth fifty cents.

16. A dollar is worth one hundred pennies.

EXERCISES

A. What time is it?

1.

2.

3.

4.

5.

6.

7.

8.

9.

10.

11.

12.

B. Answer the questions in complete sentences. Answer questions 1 through 12 according to your personal experience.

1. During the week, what time do you usually get up in the morning?

2. What time do you leave your house?

3. What time do you arrive at work or school?

4. What time do you have lunch every day?

5. What time does your English class begin?

6. What time does your English class end?

7. What time do you usually get home in the evening?

8. What time do you eat dinner?

9. What time do you go to bed?

10. On the weekends, what time do you usually get up in the morning?

11. On the weekends, what time do you usually go to bed?

12. What time is it now?

13. In the picture, is it 7 A.M. or 7 P.M.?

14. In the picture, is it noon or midnight?

15. What time does the play begin?

16. What time does it end?

C. Answer the questions in complete sentences.

1. How much is a nickel worth?

2. What is the name of the ten-cent coin?

3. How much is a penny worth?

4. What is the name of the twenty-five-cent coin?

5. Which coin is worth fifty cents?

6. What are dollars usually made of?

7. How many cents are there in a dollar?

8. Here are five different coins. What are their names?

NEW WORDS

after	different	go to bed	paper
arrive	dime	half	past
A.M.	dollar	leave	penny
be worth	during	make	P.M.
cent	end (v)	metal	quarter
clock	get home	midnight	time
coin	get up	nickel	weekend

24 PAST TENSE:
to be—Affirmative

I	was		we	were
you	were		you	were
he				
she	was		they	were
it				

1. Today is Wednesday. Yesterday was Tuesday.

2. On Monday and Tuesday the weather was very bad.

3. I was absent from school yesterday.

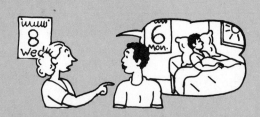

4. You were absent on Monday.

. My cousin Ann was at school both days. Andy was there, too.

. You and I were absent from school two days last week.

. You and your cousin were absent last Friday.

. Nancy and Bob were absent last Thursday. They were sick, too.

. We were all outside together last Saturday and Sunday. The weather was beautiful.

EXERCISES

A. Substitute the subject in the sentence.

Example: He was sick yesterday.　　　　they
They were sick last weekend.

1.	he	5.	Michael	9.	my friends
2.	she and I	6.	she	10.	I
3.	we	7.	your teacher	11.	you and I
4.	you	8.	Mr. Harris	12.	both of you

B. Change the verbs in the sentences to the past tense. Make any other necessary changes in adverbs.

1. Today is Tuesday.
   Yesterday was Monday.

2. I'm sick today.

3. You're late today.

4. Mrs. Ross is at home today.

5. Joan and her brother are here.

6. The book is on my desk.

7. You and your cousin are both sick.

8. Jack is at his sister's house.

9. We're in the restaurant.

10. They're in school today.

C. Answer the questions in complete sentences.

. What day of the week was yesterday?
Yesterday was Thursday.

. Where were Donna and Frank last night?

. Were you and your brother at home this morning?

. Was Diane late this morning?

Were Henry and Lee at your house last week?

6. Were you outside on Saturday?

7. Was the weather hot or cold on
   Monday?

8. Was Joe sick last weekend?

9. Was Sue in her office on Friday?

10. Was the weather good or bad
    yesterday?

1. What day was I absent from school last week?

2. Where were you on Sunday?

3. Was he at his friend's house yesterday?

4. Were they at the library on Saturday?

NEW WORDS

absent	friend	sick	very
all	last	Sunday	was
beautiful	Monday	Thursday	weather
cousin	outside	today	Wednesday
Friday	Saturday	Tuesday	were
			yesterday

25 PAST TENSE:
to be—Negative and Questions

Form the past tense negative of *to be* by placing *not* after the verb.

FULL FORMS				CONTRACTED FORMS			
I	was not	we	were not	I	wasn't	we	weren't
you	were not	you	were not	you	weren't	you	weren't
he she it	was not	they	were not	he she it	wasn't	they	weren't

Form past tense questions by placing the past tense forms of *to be* before the subject.

Was	I . . . . ?	Were we . . . ?
Were	you . . ?	Were you . . ?
Was	he . . . ? she . . ? it . . . . ?	Were they . . ?

1. Was I very late yesterday?
   No, you weren't.

2. Were you out of town last week?
   No, I wasn't.

. Was Louis at your house last night?
No, he wasn't.

. Was your wife at home this morning?
No, she wasn't.

. Were we helpful?
No, you weren't.

. Were you and your husband angry
because I was late?
No, we weren't.

. Were your parents tired after their
trip?
No, they weren't.

EXERCISES

A. Substitute the subject in the sentence.

Example: We weren't tired yesterday.   Elizabeth
Elizabeth wasn't tired yesterday.

1. I
2. Bob and Ann
3. you (singular)
4. Peter

5. he
6. their sister
7. his wife
8. your parents

9. they
10. you (plural)
11. his brother
12. she

B. Substitute the subjects listed in exercise A in this question.

Example: Was he out of town last week?   Elizabeth
Was Elizabeth out of town last week?

C. Change the sentences to questions and then to the negative.

1. Gil was at home on Monday.
Was Gil at home on Monday?
Gil wasn't at home on Monday.

2. Yesterday was Tuesday.

3. Chris was at their house for dinner last night.

4. It was very windy yesterday.

5. My husband was sick last week.

6. You and your children were in Chicago last month.

7. Jack and Ed were always good friends.

8. Ray was in the restaurant at noon.

9. They were here this morning.

10. We were happy to see them.

D. Answer the questions in complete sentences.

1. Was the weather good or bad
yesterday?
The weather was bad yesterday.

2. Was your cousin sick last week?

3. Was I on time or late?

. Were you all at your desks at ten
o'clock?

. Were your friends at the library?

6. Were you at home or at work this morning?

7. Was your teacher old or young?

8. Was Richie absent on Friday?

9. Were they out of town or at home on the weekend?

10. Was it raining or snowing yesterday?

1. Was it windy last night?

2. Was she a cook or a taxi driver in her first job?

3. Was the teacher angry because you were late?

4. Were you at Peggy's party or at home last night?

NEW WORDS

angry	first	out	town
because	helpful	parents	trip
cook	husband	party	wife
driver	job	tired	windy

131

26 PAST TENSE:
Regular Verbs—Affirmative

For most regular verbs, add *-ed.*

wait	waited*
listen	listened
walk	walked**

I	walked	we	walked
you	walked	you	walked
he she it	walked	they	walked

For verbs ending in *e,* add *-d.*

arrive	arrived
close	closed

For most verbs ending in a vowel followed by *y,* add *-ed.*

enjoy	enjoyed
play	played
stay	stayed

For some verbs ending in a vowel followed by *y,* change the *y* to *i* and add *-d.*

say	said
pay	paid
lay	laid

For verbs ending in a consonant followed by *y,* change the *y* to *i* and add *-ed.*

study	studied
try	tried

For verbs ending in *nd* and *ld,* change the final *d* to *t.*

send	sent
lend	lent
spend	spent
build	built

*Most verbs ending in a *t* or the sound *t* pronounce the past tense *-d* or *-ed* as an extra syllable: *wait—waited, hate—hated.*

**Most verbs ending in a *k* or the sound *k* pronounce the past tense *-ed* as the sound *t: walk—walked, like—liked.*

1. I waited for you until five o'clock.

2. You arrived too late for the meeting.

3. Paula enjoyed the lecture last night.

4. Tom stayed home all last week.

5. It rained all day yesterday.

6. We paid our rent and all of our bills.

7. You and Lee lent her ten dollars.

8. The carpenters built that bookcase.

EXERCISES

A. Change the verbs in the sentences to the past tense.

1. I study my English lesson every night.
   I studied my English lesson every night.

2. They visit us every day.

3. He always wants to travel with us.

4. Every day we ask questions and learn new things.

5. You and Hazel stay home every night.

6. I walk to work at eight in the morning.

7. She pays the rent every month.

8. You arrive late every day.

9. We always enjoy the class.

10. They pay their bills on time.

11. My brother always lends me money.

12. I usually enjoy the lectures.

13. It always rains in the afternoon.

14. Sara and I play tennis every week.

15. Larry sends the letters in the morning.

16. She always opens the door and he always closes it.

17. Her friends always wait for her.

18. The teacher explains the lesson to the students.

19. They live in the United States.

20. That book belongs to me.

3. Fill in the blanks with the past tense of the verb(s) in parentheses.

1. I ___arrived___ at nine o'clock this morning. (arrive)

2. We _____ an hour for you. (wait)

3. Walt and I _____ at home and _____ television. (stay, watch)

4. I _____ the money and he _____ it. (send, spend)

5. I _____ my lesson and _____ all the questions. (study, answer)

6. A new store ＿＿＿＿＿＿＿ last week. (open)

7. You ＿＿＿＿＿＿＿ on First Street. (live)

8. You ＿＿＿＿＿＿＿ Mieko with her English lessons. (help)

9. Don and Lee ＿＿＿＿＿＿＿ me yesterday. (visit)

10. We ＿＿＿＿＿ a new house. (build)

1. A tall man _____ into the hospital. (walk)

2. The teacher _____ us questions in Spanish. (ask)

3. It _____ hard last night. (rain)

4. They _____ to us about their trip to South America. (talk)

New Words

answer (v)	enjoy	lay	say
ask	hard	lend	spend
bill	help (v)	listen to	stay
bookcase	hospital	meeting	try
build	hour	question	until
carpenter	into	rent	wait

27 PAST TENSE:
Irregular Verbs—Affirmative

A verb is irregular when it has its own past tense form. That form is the same for all persons.

I	saw	we	saw
you	saw	you	saw
he she it	saw	they	saw

Learn these irregular verbs and their past tense forms. See the Appendix on page 222 for a list of common irregular verbs.

PRESENT	PAST	PRESENT	PAST
begin	began	know	knew
bring	brought	leave	left
buy	bought	make	made
come	came	put	put
do	did	read	read*
drink	drank	run	ran
drive	drove	see	saw
eat	ate	sell	sold
fall	fell	sing	sang
feel	felt	sit	sat
forget	forgot	sleep	slept
get	got	speak	spoke
give	gave	stand	stood
go	went	take	took
have	had	teach	taught
hear	heard	wear	wore
		write	wrote

*The past tense of *to read* is pronounced like the word *red*.

On Monday my day began very early. I got up at six o'clock.

2. I left home at 6:45, drove to work, and got there at 7:45.

The trip took an hour because of the heavy traffic.

4. At 9:00 my assistant brought me the mail and put some telephone messages on my desk.

I read the mail and wrote answers to some of the letters.

6. At noon I ate lunch with a client. We went to a local restaurant.

I had an appointment at 2:00 and saw several clients during the rest of the afternoon.

8. When I reached home, I felt very tired. I slept well that night.

EXERCISES

A. Change the verbs in the sentences to the past tense. Change *every* to *last*. Change *every day* to *yesterday*.

1. I see James every Monday.
   I saw James last Monday.

2. He sits in that chair every week.

3. We write a lot of letters every week.

4. Alice brings her lunch every Friday.

5. Vince and Barbie eat in the cafeteria every day.

6. You and Rosanna get good seats every night.

7. That man comes in and buys an orange every Thursday.

8. They drink a lot of milk every day.

9. I read the newspaper every night.

10. He brings his books to school every day.

11. I go to the movies every Saturday night.

12. They get on the bus at 8:00 every Monday morning.

13. We do our homework together every night.

14. Cindy teaches twenty-five classes every week.

15. The young boy sleeps late every Sunday morning.

16. I speak to that client every day.

17. She sells newspapers every day.

18. I put many pencils in the drawer every week.

19. They read every night.

20. The little girl runs home from school every day.

Fill in the blanks with the past tense of the verb(s) in parentheses.

My father _____*bought*_____ cherries yesterday. (buy)

The salesclerk _____ us some strawberries and we _____ them home. (sell, take)

She _____ us her telephone number. (give)

The waiter _____ our dinner. (bring)

The child _____ down the street and _____ . (run, fall)

6. When he _____ the
   police, he _____ around
   the corner. (see, run)

7. She _____ a newspaper
   and _____ her milk.
   (read, drink)

8. Amy and Rob _____ to our
   house for dinner last night. (come)

9. I _____ to close the
   windows. (forget)

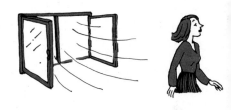

10. They _____ their
    children on a trip. (take)

1. He _____ to me about the problem. (speak)

2. Ellen _____ until ten o'clock this morning. (sleep)

3. We _____ our boots yesterday when it _____ . (wear, rain)

4. Last night I _____ music from the street all night. (hear)

NEW WORDS

afternoon	busy	hear	rest
answer	cafeteria	local	salesclerk
appointment	client	message	several
around	come	music	traffic
assistant	corner	problem	wear
bring	fall (v)	reach	

28 PAST TENSE: *Regular and Irregular Verbs—Negative*

Form the negative past tense by placing *did not (didn't)* before the base form of the verb.

I didn't walk to school.   *I walked to the office.*
She didn't see Marco.   *She saw Maria.*

FULL FORMS		CONTRACTED FORMS	
I did not see	we did not see	I didn't see	we didn't see
you did not see	you did not see	you didn't see	you didn't see
he she } did not see it	they did not see	he she } didn't see it	they didn't see

1. I bought a lot of food, but I didn't buy any cheese.

2. You spoke to us last week, but you didn't speak to us yesterday.

3. Carlo saw her in the park last Sunday, but she didn't see him.

4. Betty left work at 5:00 on Tuesday, but Peter didn't leave until 7:00.

5. It rained all weekend, but it didn't rain on Monday.

6. Jack and I played tennis every morning last week, but we didn't play this morning.

7. You and Maria did your homework every night last week, but you didn't do it last night.

8. Ruth and Nick went somewhere on Thursday, but they didn't go anywhere on Friday.*

*A negative verb plus *anywhere* is the opposite of *somewhere*. Any, anyone, anywhere, anything are usually used in negative and interrogative sentences; some, someone, somewhere, something are usually used in affirmative sentences.

EXERCISES

A. Change the sentences to the negative. Use the new subject in parentheses and use contractions.

1. I saw you yesterday. (Bill)
   Bill didn't see you yesterday.

2. You heard the answer. (I)

3. He looked for you. (she)

4. She arrived at five o'clock. (you)

5. I taught two classes last night. (Mr. Rose)

6. We went home early yesterday. (they)

7. You and Fred spent too much money. (Joe and I)

8. She brought a friend with her. (Mrs. Jackson)

9. They drank milk because they were thirsty. (we)

10. I wore a coat yesterday because it was cold. (he)

B. Answer the questions in complete sentences. First give an affirmative answer and then a negative answer.

1. Did you and Bob drive or walk to work yesterday?
   Bob and I walked to work yesterday.
   We didn't drive to work.

2. Did their plane arrive late or on time?

. Did you see Ron or Charles yesterday?

. Did she write letters or visit the zoo on Sunday?

. Did I give you that book last week or did I forget it?

. Did you or Harriet pay for our cold drinks?

New Words

anywhere	on time
cheese	somewhere
drink	zoo

29 PAST TENSE: *Regular and Irregular Verbs—Questions*

Form questions in the past tense by placing *did* in front of the subject. Use the base form of the verb. Notice the short answer.

Did you walk to the office?   *Yes, we did. We walked to the office this morning.*
Did she see Maria?   *Yes, she did. She saw Maria yesterday.*

Did I see . . . . . ?	Did we see . . . . . ?
Did you see . . . ?	Did you see . . . . ?
Did { he / she / it } see . . ?	Did they see . . . ?

1. What did you do yesterday?
   We went on a picnic.

2. Where did you go?
   We went to a beautiful park.

3. Did you bring a lot of food?
   Yes, we brought sandwiches,
   hamburgers, and frankfurters.

What else did you bring?
We also brought some soft drinks and
a few bottles of mineral water.

Did you play tennis?
No, we played baseball.

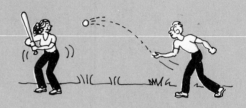

Did you go for a walk in the park?
Yes, we did, and we found a waterfall.

What time did you get home?
We got home at ten o'clock last night.

Did you have a good time?
Yes, we had a great time.

EXERCISES

A. Write questions for these answers. Use the new subject in parentheses.

1. I worked late last night. (you)
   Did you work late last night?

2. Susan brought her lunch with her. (Ana)

3. We saw Judy in the restaurant. (you)

4. He forgot to close the kitchen door. (they)

5. They sat near her at school. (Joe)

6. John went to Mexico on his vacation. (you)

7. They left for Los Angeles yesterday. (Bill and Maria)

8. We put our books on the desk. (they)

9. She spoke to the teacher in Spanish. (you)

10. They ate dinner with their parents. (Andy and Sue)

11. You arrived on time this morning. (she)

12. He sent them the letter last week. (Alan)

B. Answer in complete sentences according to your personal experience.

1. What time did you get up this morning?

2. What time did you go to bed last night?

3. Where did you have lunch yesterday?

4. What did you eat for lunch yesterday?

5. What did you do last night?

6. What else did you do last night?

NEW WORDS

a few	find	mineral water
also	frankfurter	picnic
bottle	great	soft drink
else	hamburger	waterfall

30 REVIEW

Andy's Friday Schedule

A. Look at the pictures. Using the past tense, write ten sentences about Andy's activities on Friday.

Example: *At six thirty on Friday morning, Andy got up.*

B. Now imagine that you're watching a movie of Andy's activities on Friday. Write ten sentences about what he's doing as you watch him. Use the continuous present tense.

Example: 1. *He's getting up.*

C. Change your sentences in exercise B to the negative.

Example: 1. *He's not getting up.*   or   *He isn't getting up.*

D. Ask questions to correspond with the underlined words in each of the answers below. Use the word in parentheses to begin the question.

. Nancy got up at <u>seven o'clock</u> on Monday. (when)
When did Nancy get up on Monday?

. <u>Nancy</u> ate breakfast at seven thirty. (who)

. Nancy went to <u>her friend's house.</u> (where)

. Nancy is wearing <u>a new dress.</u> (what)

. <u>No</u>, Nancy didn't eat breakfast on Sunday. (did)

. <u>Yes</u>, Nancy is studying Spanish now. (is)

E. Draw lines to connect the corresponding subject and possessive pronouns. Then make two sentences, one in the past and one in the continuous present tense, using each pair.

you	her
Alex	your
Margo and I	his
she	our
you and Tony	your

You ate your breakfast. You're eating your breakfast.

31 ADJECTIVES AND ADVERBS

An adjective modifies a noun:

An adverb modifies a verb, an adjective, or another adverb:

a *bad* answer
a *tall building*

You answered *badly*.
You answered *very* badly.

Many adverbs are formed by adding *-ly* to the adjective.

They are *quick* workers.
She is a *beautiful* singer.
He's a *bad* tennis player.

They work *quickly*.
She sings *beautifully*.
He plays tennis *badly*.

Some adjectives ending in a consonant plus *-y* form the adverb by changing the *-y* to *i* and adding *-ly*.

It's an *easy* English class.

We learn English *easily*.

Some adjectives and adverbs have the same form.

This is *hard* work.
They are *fast* workers.

You work *hard*.
They work *fast*.*

Some words ending in *-ly* can be either adjectives or adverbs.

I have an *early* class.
He has a *weekly* baseball game.

I always go to class *early*.
He plays baseball *weekly*.

The adverb corresponding to the adjective *good* is *well*.

Ana is a *good* worker.

She works *well*.

Some adverbs do not have an adjective form: *here, now, then, soon, too, far, near, always, seldom, never, too.*

Adverbs of frequency come before the verb, except with the verb *to be*.

He's *always* hungry.
He *never* eats a big breakfast.
They're *never* late.
They *usually* come early.

*The adverbs *fast* and *quickly* are synonyms.

1. Andrew is a *careful* student.
   He does his homework *carefully*.

2. Dee gave the *correct* answer.
   She answered the question *correctly*.

3. You have a *soft* voice, not a *loud* voice.
   You speak *softly*, not *loudly*.

4. This is a *fast* plane.
   It moves *fast*.

5. This was a *hard* lesson.
   I worked *hard* on this lesson.

6. I waited a *long* time for the bus.
   Did you wait *long*?

7. Valerie is a *good* swimmer.
   She swims *well*.

8. I *sometimes* forget my phone number.
   I'm *sometimes* forgetful.

EXERCISES

A. Fill in the blanks with *good* or *well*.

1. That man is a ___*good*___ singer. He sings very ___*well*___ .

2. You swim very _____ . You're a very _____ swimmer.

3. Karen plays baseball _____ . She's a _____ baseball player.

4. They did _____ on the exam. They're _____ students.

5. Arlene is a _____ teacher. She explains the lessons _____ .

6. Victor cooks _____ . He's a _____ cook.

7. I'm a _____ typist. I type very _____ .

8. Karen is a _____ artist. She draws _____ .

3. Use the correct form of the word in parentheses.

   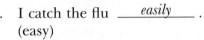

1. I catch the flu ___easily___ .
(easy)

2. You arrived at school
_____ . (late)

3. Elaine sings _____ .
(beautiful)

4. He's a very _____ student.
(careful)

5. I didn't answer the question
_____ . (correct)

6. Barry wrote his exercises
_____ . (quick)

NEW WORDS

careful	exam	player	sometimes
catch (v)	fast	quick	swimmer
correct	flu	really	type (v)
draw	forgetful	report	well
early	loud	singer	
easy	phone	soft	

32 ADJECTIVES AND ADVERBS: *Comparative Forms*

The comparative form of adjectives and adverbs shows the difference between two people or things. This form is always followed by *than*.

ADJECTIVES

Most one-syllable and some two-syllable adjectives add *-er* to form the comparative.

> It's warm. It's *warmer than* yesterday. Yesterday was *cooler than* today.
> Jane is tall. She's *taller than* Joe. Joe is *shorter than* Jane.

Some adjectives ending in a consonant plus *-y* change the *-y* to *i* and add *-er*.

> She's a happy person. She's *happier than* me.

Some one-syllable adjectives double the final consonant.

> They have a big house. It's *bigger than* mine.

Some two-syllable adjectives and all three-syllable adjectives form the comparative with *more* or *less*.

> I'm careful. I'm *more careful than* you. You're *less careful than* me. My book is interesting.
> It's *more interesting than* yours. Yours is *less interesting than* mine.

A few adjectives have special comparative forms.

> It's a good day. It's *better than* yesterday. It's a bad day. It's *worse than* yesterday.

ADVERBS

Compare adverbs in the same way as adjectives.

> Joe came early. He came *earlier than* me. I came *later than* Joe.
> I eat slowly. I eat *more slowly than* you. You eat *more quickly than* me.

A few adverbs have special comparative forms.

> You play baseball well. You play *better than* me. I play baseball badly. I play *worse than* you

ADJECTIVES AND ADVERBS

To show similarity between two things or people, use *as* before and after the adjectives or adverbs.

> Artie is *as tall as* Peggy. Jackie runs *as quickly as* Mike.

1. Alice's hair is longer than Pat's.

2. This lesson is less difficult than that one. It's easier!

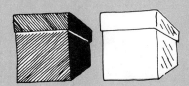

3. The black box is as large as the white one.

4. Henry is a better student than his brother Don.

5. Sarah is a worse musician than Larry.

6. The plane arrived earlier than the boat.

7. Dogs run more slowly than horses.

8. Kay plays chess better than Paul.

EXERCISES

A.   Answer the questions in complete sentences.

1. Who runs more quickly, Sam or
   Sandra?
   Sam runs as quickly as Sandra.

2. Are giraffes taller or shorter than
   lions?

3. Is Lucy older or younger than Steve?

4. Is the white house larger or smaller
   than the gray one?

5. Does Richard do his homework faster
   or more slowly than his sister?

6. Do you usually get home earlier or later than your husband?

7. Which runs less quickly, a turtle or a cat?

8. Is Carol's bag heavier or lighter than Robert's suitcase?

9. Is the black car newer or older than the white one?

0. Who is taller, Lee or Ann?

B. Fill in the blanks using the comparative form of the adjective or adverb in parentheses.

1. South Street is __*wider than*__ North Avenue. (wide)

2. Phil sings _____ Linda. (bad)

3. Linda dances _____ Phil. (well)

4. Rabbits run _____ turtles. (fast)

5. The tree is _____ the house. (tall)

. You do your homework
_____ Joey. (carefully)

. This book is _____ that
one. (interesting)

. Pam is a _____ tennis
player _____ Patrick. (good)

. The weather today is
_____ yesterday. (bad)

New Words

bag	giraffe	large	north	turtle
better	gray	less	slow	wide
chess	hair	lion	south	worse
difficult	interesting	more	than	

33 ADJECTIVES AND ADVERBS:
Superlative Forms

ADJECTIVES

The superlative form of adjectives compares three or more people or things. This form is always preceded by *the*.

Most one-syllable and some two-syllable adjectives add *-est* to form the superlative. They add *-st* to adjectives that end in *-e*.

> That street is wide.
> It is wider than my street.
> It's the *widest* street of all.

Some two-syllable adjectives and all three-syllable adjectives form the superlative by using *the most* or *the least*.

> Joe is intelligent.
> Jay is more intelligent than Joe. Joe is less intelligent than Jay.
> Jim is *the most intelligent* of all. Joe is *the least intelligent* of all.

A few adjectives have special superlative forms.

> She's a good teacher. He's a bad student.
> She's a better teacher than Jane. He's a worse student than Al.
> She's *the best* teacher in the school. He's *the worst* student in the school.

ADVERBS

Adverbs form the superlative in the same way as adjectives.

> Sue arrived early. You arrived late.
> Sue arrived earlier than you. You arrived later than Sue.
> Sue arrived *the earliest* of all. You arrived *the latest* of all.

A few adverbs have special superlative forms.

> Ann dances well. Dave dances badly.
> Ann dances better than Dave. Dave dances worse than Ann.
> Ann dances *the best* of all. Dave dances *the worst* of all.

. Here are three circles. The first circle is larger than the second circle. The second circle is smaller than the first circle and is larger than the third circle. The first circle is the largest, and the third circle is the smallest of the three.

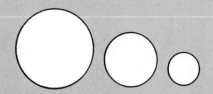

. The first cat is thinner than the second cat. The second cat is thinner than the third cat. The third cat is the fattest of all. The first cat is the thinnest of all.

. Peter is a better cook than Jean. Jean is a better cook than Carl. Carl is the worst cook of all, and Peter is the best.

. Bicycles are less expensive than cars. Cars are less expensive than trucks. Trucks are the most expensive, and bicycles are the least expensive of the three.

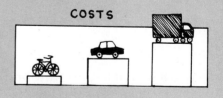

. In the United States, January and February are the coldest months of the year, and July and August are the hottest.

EXERCISE

Answer the questions in complete sentences.

1. Which circle is the largest? Which one
   is the smallest?
   The second circle is the largest, and the first
   one is the smallest.

first   second   third

2. Which is the largest animal of the
   three?

3. Which one travels the fastest: a bus, a
   train, or a plane?

4. In the United States, are July and
   August the coldest or the hottest
   months of the year?

5. Who is the worst cook of the three?

COSTS

5. Which one is the least expensive?

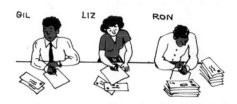

GIL   LIZ   RON

7. Who wrote the most letters?

SEVENTH ST.
SIXTH ST.
FIFTH ST.
FOURTH ST.

8. Which street is the widest?

9. Which animal is the most interesting?

New Words

August	fat	July	narrow	third
best	February	least	quiet	truck
circle	intelligent	month	second	worst
expensive	January	most	thin	year

34 FUTURE TENSE WITH *WILL:*
Affirmative

The future tense with *will* expresses a simple future action, a promise, or determination. It is formed by placing *will* before the verb.

> *I'll tell you tomorrow.*
> *We'll see you at seven o'clock.*

FULL FORMS		CONTRACTED FORMS	
I will walk	we will walk	I'll walk	we'll walk
you will walk	you will walk	you'll walk	you'll walk
he		he'll	
she } will walk	they will walk	she'll } walk	they'll walk
it		it'll	

1. Tomorrow Phil will get up at about seven o'clock.

2. First he'll wash his hands and face.

3. Next he'll brush his teeth.

4. Then he'll comb his hair.

5. Then he'll get dressed.

6. At seven thirty he'll have breakfast.

7. His brother and sister will have breakfast with him.

8. At eight o'clock he'll leave for work.

9. He and I will probably meet on the corner near his home.

10. If it's raining, we'll take the bus to work.

11. If the weather is good, we'll walk.

12. We'll arrive at the office at about a quarter to nine.

13. He'll probably have lunch alone.

14. At five o'clock we'll go home.

EXERCISES

A. Change the sentences to the future tense. Change *this* to *next*. Change *every* to *tomorrow*.

1. We're studying English this year.
   We'll study English next year.
2. She speaks English well this month.
3. I'm a good student this week.
4. They eat lunch with us every afternoon.
5. She sits next to me in school every evening.
6. He meets me on the corner every morning.
7. They eat dinner in a restaurant every evening.
8. I'm getting us some soft drinks this Saturday.
9. He brushes his teeth and combs his hair every morning.
10. You walk to school every morning.

B. Answer the questions in complete sentences. Answer questions 1 through 8 according to your personal experience.

1. What time will you get up tomorrow?
2. What time will you have breakfast?
3. Will you have breakfast alone or with your family?
4. What will you probably eat for breakfast tomorrow morning?
5. Where will you eat lunch tomorrow?
6. What will you do tomorrow evening?
7. What time will you have dinner?
8. What time will you go to bed?

9. Where will Ruth go tomorrow?

10. What time will she get there?

11. What will she do tomorrow afternoon?

12. What time will she have dinner?

NEW WORDS

about	face	later	then
alone	get dressed	next	tomorrow
brush (v)	hand	probably	will
comb (v)	if		

35 FUTURE TENSE WITH *WILL:*
Negative and Questions

The negative of the future tense places *not* after *will.* Notice the irregular contracted form *won't.*

FULL FORMS		CONTRACTED FORMS	
I will not go	we will not go	I won't go	we won't go
you will not go	you will not go	you won't go	you won't go
he } she } will not go it }	they will not go	he } she } won't go it }	they won't go

Questions in the future tense place *will* before the subject.

Will	I go?	Will we go?
Will	you go?	Will you go?
Will	{ he { she } go? { it	Will they go?

1. If I leave home at six o'clock, will I
   arrive on time at the party?
   No, you won't.

2. Will you go to the library on Friday?
   No, I won't.

3. Will Roger go on the picnic tomorrow?
   No, he won't

Will it rain tomorrow?
No, it won't.

Will Ken and I need reservations for
the show tonight?
No, you won't.

Will you and Martha go to the beach if
it rains?
No, we won't.

Will Fred and Norma leave the city on
Saturday?
No, they won't.

EXERCISES

A. Change the sentences to questions, and then answer them in the negative using complete sentences.

1. I'll return tomorrow.
   Will you return tomorrow?
   No, I won't return tomorrow.

2. They'll leave the city at ten o'clock tonight.

3. The weather will be good tomorrow.

4. We'll stay home if it rains.

5. They'll have a good time next week.

6. Jerry will lend us the money tomorrow.

7. He'll wait for us until tonight.

8. We'll watch the animals in the zoo.

9. Rachel will help us tonight.

10. You'll come here again.

B. Answer the questions in complete sentences. First give an affirmative answer and then a negative answer.

1. Will you buy a house or an apartment?
   I'll buy a house.
   I won't buy an apartment.

2. Will they meet me at the bus station or at the hotel?

Will they drink milk or coffee?

Will they arrive before or after noon?

Will the children swim in the ocean or in a pool?

Will he set the table for three or four people?

NEW WORDS

apartment	meet	pool	show
beach	need (v)	reservation	station
here	ocean	set (v)	tonight
hotel			

36 REFLEXIVE AND INTENSIVE PRONOUNS

Subject Pronoun	Reflexive/Intensive Pronoun	Subject Pronoun	Reflexive/Intensive Pronoun
I	myself	we	ourselves
you	yourself	you	yourselves
he	himself		
she	herself	they	themselves
it	itself		

REFLEXIVE PRONOUNS

Reflexive pronouns show that both the subject and the object of a verb are the same person or thing.

> *He* shaves *himself* every morning.
> *She* hurt *herself* yesterday.

Reflexive pronouns are often the objects of prepositions.

> *Paula* is looking *at herself* in the mirror.
> *Tony* cooks breakfast *for himself*.

Reflexive pronouns used with *by* mean "alone" or "without help."

> *I* always eat lunch *by myself*.
> The *girl* lifted that heavy box *by herself*.

INTENSIVE PRONOUNS

Intensive pronouns stress the importance of the noun or pronoun to which they refer.

> I phoned the *President himself*.
> *They themselves* built their whole house.

Intensive pronouns usually appear directly after the subject or at the end of the sentence.

> *I myself* will buy the videodisc.
> I will buy the videodisc *myself*.

REFLEXIVE PRONOUNS

Martha cut herself with the scissors.

2. I burned myself with a match.

The children are five years old.* They get dressed by themselves every morning.

4. After breakfast they go to school by themselves.

INTENSIVE PRONOUNS

Of course he was here; I myself saw him.

6. You yourself told me! Don't you remember?

If you both have time, you can paint the house yourselves.

8. That doctor says that smoking is bad, but he himself smokes.

*otice that age is expressed with the verb *to be*.

EXERCISES

A. Fill in the blanks with the correct reflexive or intensive pronouns.

1. I saw _____*myself*_____ in the mirror.

2. The dog sits by _____ in the corner.

3. The little boy got dressed by _____ .

4. They want to study by _____ .

5. She found _____ alone in a big city.

6. You and Mary run this business

    _____ .

7. I gave him those videodiscs

    _____ .

8. We always eat by _____ .

9. He _____ gave me the
   book.

10. The cook hurt _____
    with her own knife.

B. Answer the questions in complete sentences.

1. Did she make that dress herself?
   Yes, she made that dress herself.

2. Did he himself give you that address?

3. Did they come by themselves?

4. Do you prefer to go to the movies by yourself or with someone?

5. Did the child hurt himself when he fell?

Does the cat take care of itself?

Did you yourself mail the letter?

Does she like to walk by herself in the park?

Do you cook for yourselves in the evening?

New Words

...ddress	himself	myself	remember	someone
...rn (v)	hurt (v)	of course	scissors	tell
...siness	itself	ourselves	shave (v)	videodisc
...re	lift (v)	own	smoke (v)	yourself
...t (v)	match	paint (v)	smoking	yourselves
...rself	mirror			

37 FUTURE TENSE WITH *GOING TO*: *Affirmative*

The future tense with *going to* expresses a simple future action, but it generally indicates that the action is planned and will occur in the immediate future. It is formed with the present tense of *to be* followed by *going* plus the infinitive of the main verb.

Why are you taking off your shoes?   *Because I'm going to go to bed.**

FULL FORMS		CONTRACTED FORMS	
I am going to eat	we are going to eat	I'm going to eat	we're going to eat
you are going to eat	you are going to eat	you're going to eat	you're going to eat
he ⎫		he's ⎫	
she ⎬ is going to eat	they are going to eat	she's ⎬ going to eat	they're going to eat
it ⎭		it's ⎭	

1. I'm going to see a movie tonight.

2. You're going to be late for the opera.

*The future tense with *going to* often omits the main verb *to go*. What are you going to do now? I'm going to bed. (I'm going to go to bed.)

He's going to be an astronaut when he grows up.

She's going to have chocolate ice cream for dessert.

We're going to play tennis this afternoon.

You're going to need your umbrellas soon.

They're going to travel to Japan on their vacation.

EXERCISES

Substitute the subject in the sentence. Use contractions when possible.

      Example: He's going to arrive soon.   you
                     You're going to arrive soon.

1. we	5. our teacher	9. you
2. Fran and I	6. the woman	10. the people
3. he	7. the men	11. you and Joh▸
4. the plane	8. they	12. Laura

B. Change the sentences to the *going to* future.

1. He's waiting for us.
   He's going to wait for us.

2. She studied French.

3. They met us after class.

4. He's four years old.

5. The teacher will give us an exam tomorrow.

6. We're playing tennis.

7. She had strawberry ice cream for dessert.

8. You and Paul brought sandwiches and fruit to the picnic.

9. I bought some new clothes.

10. You and your brother went to the opera.

C. Answer the questions in complete sentences.

1. What's your sister going to study?
She's going to study biology.

2. Which cities are his parents going to visit?

. Is your father going to clean the house by himself?

4. Are we going to the beach or to the mountains for the weekend?

. Is Margaret going to be a doctor or a dentist when she grows up?

6. What time are they going to meet us?

NEW WORDS

astronaut	clothes	mountain	take off
biology	dessert	opera	vacation
clean (v)	grow up	soon	

38 FUTURE TENSE WITH *GOING TO:*
Negative and Questions

The negative form of the future tense with *going to* uses the negative forms of *to be* plus *going* plus the infinitive.

FULL FORMS

I	am not going to eat	we are not going to eat
you	are not going to eat	you are not going to eat
he		
she	is not going to eat	they are not going to eat
it		

CONTRACTED FORMS

I'm	not going to eat	we aren't going to eat
you	aren't* going to eat	you aren't going to eat
he		
she	isn't going to eat	they aren't going to eat
it		

Future tense questions with *going to* place *to be* before the subject.

Am	I	going to eat?	Are we	going to eat?
Are	you	going to eat?	Are you	going to eat?
Is	he / she / it	going to eat?	Are they going to eat?	

Short answers use a form of *to be*.

> *Are you going to fix the car yourself? Yes, I am.*

1. Are you going to take your car to the garage?
   No, I'm not.

*Remember that the alternative contractions are also possible: *you're not going to eat*, etc.

---

2. Is your uncle going to watch the
   football game tomorrow?
   No, he's not.

3. Is your cousin going to play soccer with
   you?
   No, she's not.

4. Are you and Chris going to take
   chemistry next year?
   No, we're not.

5. Are Andrea and I going to like that
   film?
   No, you're not.

6. Are your aunt and uncle going
   shopping this afternoon?
   No, they're not.

EXERCISES

A. Change the statements to questions, and then answer them in the negative using complete sentences.

1. She's going to answer your letter soon.
    Is she going to answer my letter soon?
    No, she's not going to answer your letter soon.

2. They're going to eat dinner at seven.

3. The people are going to need a reservation.

4. He's going to leave in a few minutes.

5. We're going to buy a newspaper.

6. Louis is going to cook tonight.

7. That woman is going to lend us her dictionary.

8. The children are going to play in the park.

B. Answer the questions using negative short answers.

1. Are you going out tonight?
    No, I'm not.

2. Is she going to buy a coat?

3. Are you and Eric going to take the children to the theater?

4. Are they going to bring the food for the picnic?

5. Am I going to be late?

6. Is Phil going to drive us to the train station?

7. Is it going to be cold today?

8. Are you and Jim going to China this year?

C. Write a question for each of the following answers.

1. I'm going to Chicago on my vacation.
   Where are you going on your vacation?

2. I'm going to stay at my cousin's apartment.

3. I'm going to travel there by plane.

4. Yes, she's going to meet me at the airport.

5. I'm going to give her a big bunch of flowers.

6. Then we're going to go to a soccer game.

NEW WORDS

airport	film	garage
aunt	fix	go shopping
bunch	football	soccer
chemistry	game	uncle

39 IMPERATIVE

The imperative expresses an order or command. It uses the infinitive without *to*. The subject *you* is understood.

> *Stop here and show your ID card.*

The negative uses *do not (don't)* before the verb.

> *Don't forget to meet your aunt at the airport.*

Written signs in public places use a different negative form: *no* plus the *-ing* form of the verb.*

Imperative sharpness is often softened by adding some conventional expression of courtesy: (if you) please, with your permission, if you like, if you don't mind, pardon me. . . .

> *Please wait here.*
> *Do not smoke in here, if you please.*
> *Let's close the window, if you don't mind.*
> *Pardon me; tell me if this is the fourth of July.*

1. Don't waste time. Go to school.

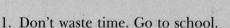

2. Wait for me. Don't walk so fast.

*The *-ing* form of a verb, when used as a noun, is called a *verbal noun* or a *gerund*.

3. Cross the street while the traffic light is green. Don't cross while the light is red.

4. Don't break your sister's toys.

5. Pay for the meal. Don't forget to leave a tip for the waiter.

6. Don't spill your coffee on my new carpet.

7. Don't stand outside in the rain. Come in!

EXERCISE

Command Hank to do each of the things that Lee does. Then ask Hank the same thing again, adding some expression of courtesy.

1. Lee isn't leaving yet; she's waiting for Jim.
   Hank, don't leave yet; wait for Jim.
   Hank, please don't leave yet; please wait for Jim.

2. Lee isn't driving too fast.

3. Lee is driving carefully.

4. Lee is crossing at the green light.

5. Lee is studying; she's not wasting time.

6. Lee is washing her hands and face.

7. Lee isn't smoking.

8. Lee is hanging up her clothes.

9. Lee is setting the table.

10. Lee isn't going out tonight.

11. Lee gets up early.

12. Lee is doing the laundry.

13. Lee doesn't spend all of her money.

14. Lee isn't lazy.

NEW WORDS

break (v)	ID card	mind (v)	please	tip
carpet	lazy	pardon	red	traffic light
cross (v)	let (v)	pay (v)	spill (v)	waste (v)
green	like (v)	permission	stop (v)	while
hang up	meal			

40 PRESENT PERFECT TENSE:
Affirmative

The present perfect tense uses the present forms of *to have* plus the past participle of the main verb. For regular verbs, the past participle form is the same as the past tense form. See the Appendix on page 222 for a list of irregular past participles.

	FULL FORMS			CONTRACTED FORMS	
I	have seen	we have seen		I've seen	we've seen
you	have seen	you have seen		you've seen	you've seen
he				he's	
she	has seen	they have seen		she's seen	they've seen
it				it's	

The present perfect tense associates past action with the present. It describes an action which has occurred at some indefinite time in the past. It sometimes describes an action completed immediately before the present. The present perfect often appears with expressions of an unfinished period of time like *recently, lately, this month,* or *this week.*

> *I've seen that movie three times.*
> *I've just had a wonderful idea.*
> *It's snowed a lot recently.*

In some cases the past action continues into the present, or might happen again.

> *I've known him for many years.* (And I still know him.)
> *She's written two novels.* (And she might write another one.)

The present perfect often appears with the time expressions *for* or *since. For* is used with a duration, or a period of time. *Since* is used with the specific date or time when the action began.

> *We've been friends for three months.*
> *We've been friends since January.*

1. I've spoken to him several times today.

2. Thank you, but I've already eaten dinner.

3. We've lived in this apartment for three years.

4. Her plane has just landed.

5. They've been friends since they were children.

EXERCISES

A. Substitute the subject in the sentence. Use contractions when possible.

Example: I've met him before.   he
        He's met him before.

1. Lee
2. Rich
3. Lee and Rich
4. we

5. they
6. she
7. you boys
8. your sister

9. you and Tracy
10. you
11. I
12. Adam and I

B. Change the verbs in italics from the past to the present perfect tense. Use contractions when possible.

1. I saw Ted and Rose.
   I've seen Ted and Rose.

2. We *bought* vegetables in the market.

3. The wind *began* to blow very hard.

4. They *drove* to work.

5. I *ate* too much.

6. She *fell* on the stairs.

7. I *wrote* to her often.

8. You *came* too late. He just *went* out.

9. He *took* the package to the post office.

10. You *were* in Miami.

11. They *went* home.

12. I *did* all the dishes.

C. Fill in the blanks with the correct present perfect form of the verb in parentheses. Use contractions when possible.

1. This is the first time you and your brother _____*have visited*_____ our farm. (visit)

2. Come into the house. It _____ to rain. (begin)

3. Our friends _____ the table for us. (set)

4. They _____ something you like. (cook)

5. The leaves* _____ from the trees. (fall)

6. I _____ that woman somewhere before. (see)

NEW WORDS

already	farm	lately	package	something
before	idea	leaf	recently	thank you
blow (v)	just	market	several	wind
do dishes	land (v)	novel	since	

The singular of *leaves* is *leaf*.

41 PRESENT PERFECT TENSE: *Negative*

The negative of the present perfect tense places *not* after *has* or *have*.

FULL FORMS		CONTRACTED FORMS	
I have not seen	we have not seen	I haven't seen	we haven't seen
you have not seen	you have not seen	you haven't seen	you haven't seen
he		he	
she } has not seen	they have not seen	she } hasn't seen	they haven't seen
it		it	

In addition to expressions of unfinished time like *recently, lately,* and *this year,* the negative of the present perfect tense may appear with *yet. Yet* indicates an action which started before the time of speaking and is still uncompleted.

> *The actor hasn't made a movie in years.*
> *We haven't had a vacation this year.*
> *I haven't done my homework yet, and my class starts in five minutes.*

1. That actress hasn't worked in a month.

2. You haven't seen my new living room and dining room furniture.

3. He hasn't asked Jane for a date yet.

4. Lois hasn't found her pocketbook yet.

5. It hasn't stopped raining all day.

6. We haven't put the new sink in the bathroom yet.

7. You and Tony haven't been to the dentist since last year.

8. They haven't found the right dresser for their bedroom.

EXERCISES

A. Substitute the subject in the sentence. Use contractions when possible.

Example: I haven't done much work lately.   he
        He hasn't done much work lately.

1. Paul and Bill
2. that student
3. you and I
4. she

5. Jeanette
6. the children
7. you
8. we

9. they
10. you and Sally
11. Patrick
12. the carpenters

B. Change the sentences to the negative.

1. She's lost her pocketbook.
   She hasn't lost her pocketbook.

2. He's finally finished his homework.

3. She's found her pocketbook.

4. They've bought many new dresses.

5. The office has closed for the day.

6. Sally has done well in her new job.

7. You and Harry have drunk all the orange juice.

8. I've spoken to him about you.

9. His parents have bought him a new bicycle.

10. He's gone home.

C. Answer the questions in complete sentences. First give an affirmative
answer and then a negative answer.

1. Have you just arrived or have
you lived here for a long time?
I've just arrived.
I haven't lived here for a long time.

2. Has Bill been sick or well
recently?

3. Has Mary gone home or to
school?

4. Has it rained or snowed here this
week?

5. Has this office been open since
January or February?

6. Have they studied French or
Spanish?

NEW WORDS

actor	date	furniture	pocketbook	stop (v)
actress	dresser	juice	right	yet
bathroom	finally	living room	sink	
bedroom	finish (v)	minute	start (v)	

42 PRESENT PERFECT TENSE: *Questions*

Present perfect tense questions place *have* or *has* before the subject.

Have I seen . . . . ?	Have we seen . . . . . ?
Have you seen . . . . . . ?	Have you seen . . . . ?
Has ⎧ he ⎫ seen . . . . . ? ⎨ she ⎬ ⎩ it ⎭	Have they seen . . . . ?

Yes/no questions with *yet* require an affirmative answer with *already* or a negative answer with *yet*. *Already* appears after *has* or *have* or at the end of the sentence. *Yet* appears at the end of the sentence.

> *Have Marty and Barbie arrived at work yet?*
> *Barbie has already arrived, but Marty hasn't arrived yet.*

Ever, meaning "at any time," is often used in present perfect tense questions. Negative answers to these questions use *never*. Affirmative answers use the simple past tense if a specific time in the past is mentioned.

> *Have you ever been late to work? No, I've never been late.*
> *Yes, I've been late twice.* or *Yes, I was late last Monday.*

1. Have I ever met your friend Liz?
   No, you've never met her.

2. Have you been to the movies recently?
   Yes, I have.

. Has he spoken to the manager about
his vacation?
Yes, he has.

. Has she finished her homework?
No, she hasn't.

. Have we paid our rent yet?
No, we haven't.

. Have you and Joan forgotten our
dinner date?
No, we haven't.

Have they written to you recently?
Yes, they have.

EXERCISES

A. **Substitute the subject in the question.**

Example: Have you ever worked in a restaurant?   Jean
        Has Jean ever worked in a restaurant?

1. Artie and Jay
2. he
3. Betty
4. that man

5. they
6. you
7. your aunt
8. you and Rob

9. she
10. Jerry
11. their son
12. those women

B. **Change the sentences to questions.**

1. I've already finished my lunch.
   Have I finished my lunch yet?

2. I've never been to South America.

3. They haven't done the dishes yet.

4. Dick has been a waiter for three years.

5. She's already finished her work.

6. That little boy has fallen every day this week.

7. Martha has spent all of her money on books.

8. He's gone for the day.

9. You've worn that dress often.

10. We've lent them the money.

11. The teacher has spoken to me about my children's work.

12. They've taken David to the beach with them.

Answer the questions in complete sentences.

1. Has Eric ever studied German?
No, Eric has never studied German.

2. Has it stopped raining yet?

3. How long has Pedro known Carmen?

4. Have they bought some records?

5. Have you eaten dinner yet?

6. Has Suzanne finished the lessons yet?

NEW WORDS

ever	never
German	records
manager	twice

43 THE CALENDAR, SEASONS, AND WEATHER

THE CALENDAR

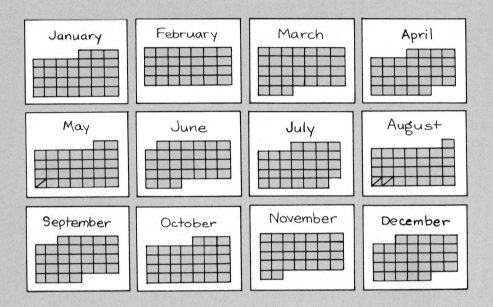

1. There are twelve months in a year: January, February, March, April, May, June, July, August, September, October, November, and December.

2. All of the months have thirty or thirty-one days, except February. February has twenty-eight days. But in a leap year February has twenty-nine days.

3. There are fifty-two weeks in a year. The days of the week are Sunday, Monday, Tuesday, Wednesday, Thursday, Friday, and Saturday.

SEASONS AND WEATHER

A year has four seasons: winter, spring, summer, and fall. Fall is sometimes called autumn.

. The winter months are December, January, and February. The weather is usually very cold. The trees are bare. Sometimes it snows a lot, and it's often very windy.

. March, April, and May are the spring months. The weather is usually warm and pleasant. Plants grow, flowers blossom, and new leaves appear on the trees.

. The summer months are June, July, and August. The weather is often very hot and very humid.

. The autumn months are September, October, and November. The weather is cool. It often rains a lot. The trees lose their leaves in the fall, and it's harvest time for many different kinds of fruits and vegetables.

EXERCISES

A. Answer the questions in complete sentences.

1. Name the months of the year.

2. How many months have thirty days? Which months are they?

3. How many months have thirty-one days? Which months are they?

4. When does February have twenty-nine days?

5. How many weeks are there in a year?

6. Name the days of the week.

7. Name the four seasons.

8. What is another name for the fall?

9. What are the names of the winter months?

10. Describe the weather in the winter.

11. Name the three months of spring.

12. How is the weather in the spring?

13. What natural changes occur in the spring?

14. Name the summer months.

15. Describe summer weather.

16. What are the names of the autumn months?

17. How is the weather in the fall?

18. What natural changes occur in the fall?

3. Answer the questions in complete sentences according to the pictures.

1. When does spring begin?
Spring begins on March 21.

2. When does summer begin?

3. When does fall begin?

4. When does winter begin?

5. What season is it in the picture?

6. What season is it in the picture?

NEW WORDS

appear	change	harvest	May	pleasant
April	cool	humid	name (v)	season
autumn	December	June	natural	September
bare	describe	leap year	November	spring
blossom (v)	except	lose	occur	summer
calendar	fall	March	October	winter

44 HOUSE AND FURNITURE

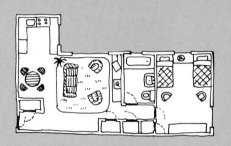

1. Carol and Jackie share a one-bedroom apartment in San Francisco. This is the floor plan.

2. The living room has some nice furniture. There are two easy chairs, a floor lamp, a television set, a record player, a VCR, and a sofa bed.

3. The dining area has a small dining room table, four chairs, and a cabinet. Carol and Jackie keep their dishes and glassware in the cabinet.

4. Their kitchen has a sink, several cabinets, and all new appliances: a stove, a refrigerator, a dishwasher, and a microwave oven.

5. Their bedroom has twin beds, a dresser, a bedside table with a lamp, and two chairs.

6. In the bathroom there's a sink, a toilet, and a bathtub with a shower.

7. The apartment has a total of four closets: two clothes closets, a linen closet, and a coat closet in the hall near the front door.

EXERCISE

Answer the questions in complete sentences.

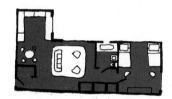

1. Name the rooms in the apartment in the picture.

2. What furniture is there in the living room?

3. What kind of sofa is there in the living room?

4. Describe the dining area.

5. What are the bathroom fixtures?

6. What furniture is there in the bedroom?

7. How many closets are there in the bedroom?

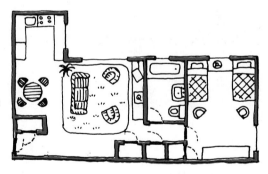

8. Name the furniture, bathroom fixtures, and kitchen appliances shown in this floor plan.

NEW WORDS

appliance	closet	hall	share (v)
area	easy chair	keep	shower
bathtub	fixture	linen	sofa bed
bed	floor plan	microwave oven	toilet
cabinet	glassware	record player	

45 REVIEW

A. Fill in the blanks with the correct form of the word in parentheses.

1. Main Street is _the widest_ of the three. (wide)

2. Lisa is _____ Pete. (tall)

3. The fifty-dollar clock is _____ of the three. (expensive)

4. Joanne arrived _____ Jim. (early)

5. They all sing very _____ . (bad)

6. In the United States, summers are _____ winters. (warm)

7. Louis is a _____ cook than Ann. (good)

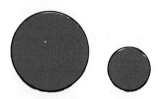

8. The second circle is _____ the first one. (small)

B. Rewrite the paragraph, changing it to the future tense with *will.* Use contractions when possible.

      Yesterday Pat and I had a happy day. She arrived at nine thirty in the morning, and she stayed for the whole day. We had breakfast together, and then we took my car to a park near my house. We had sandwiches and fresh fruit for lunch. Then we walked around the park. Did we study? No. We didn't have our books with us because we didn't have any homework. We played tennis for an hour, and then we talked and laughed a lot. It was a good day.

Tomorrow Pat and I will have a happy day.

C. Rewrite the same paragraph, using the future tense with *going to.* Make any other necessary changes. Use contractions when possible.

Tomorrow Pat and I are going to have a happy day.

D. Fill in the blanks with the correct reflexive or intensive pronouns.

1. He cut _____*himself*_____ with that knife yesterday.

2. The children hurt _____ in the park.

3. I cooked dinner for _____ this evening.

4. But, Michael, you _____ gave me those letters.

5. The little girl gets dressed by _____ every morning.

6. We built that table _____ .

7. Any and Howard study by _____ every night.

8. Did you and Tom wash the windows _____ ?

E. Change each of the sentences to a polite request.

1. We're doing our homework.
    Please do your homework.

2. I'm sitting on this chair.

3. I'm not smoking.

4. I'm not spilling the coffee.

5. We're setting the table.

6. I'm crossing the street at the corner.

7. We're waiting at the bus stop.

8. We're not forgetting to pay our bill.

F. Change the statements to questions, and then answer each question in the negative. Use the present perfect tense and contractions when possible.

1. I've already written three letters.
    Have you written any letters yet?
    No, I haven't written any letters yet.

2. We've already seen that movie.

3. She's been to California.

4. He's already left.

5. It's begun to rain.

6. They've visited us several times this week.

7. I've already found an apartment.

8. Bob and Carol have finished their homework.

G. Describe the weather in each picture. Then say the months when that kind of weather usually occurs in the United States.

It's very cold. It's snowing, and it's very windy. It's probably December, January, or February.

2.

3.

4.

H. You have just rented a new apartment. It has furniture in it. Describe the apartment to a friend.

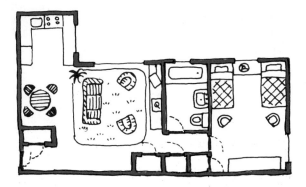

This apartment has . . .

APPENDIX

SAMPLE CONJUGATIONS

TO BE

SIMPLE PRESENT TENSE

Full Forms		Contracted Forms	
I am	we are	I'm	we're
you are	you are	you're	you're
he ⎫		he's ⎫	
she ⎬ is	they are	she's ⎬	they're
it ⎭		it's ⎭	

PAST TENSE

I was	we were
you were	you were
he ⎫	
she ⎬ was	they were
it ⎭	

FUTURE TENSE*

Full Forms		Contracted Forms	
I will be	we will be	I'll be	we'll be
you will be	you will be	you'll be	you'll be
he ⎫		he'll ⎫	
she ⎬ will be	they will be	she'll ⎬ be	they'll be
it ⎭		it'll ⎭	

PRESENT PERFECT TENSE

Full Forms		Contracted Forms	
I have been	we have been	I've been	we've been
you have been	you have been	you've been	you've been
he ⎫		he's ⎫	
she ⎬ has been	they have been	she's ⎬ been	they've been
it ⎭		it's ⎭	

*The future tense with *going to* is formed with the present tense of *to be* followed by *going* plus the infinitive of the main verb.

TO WALK

SIMPLE PRESENT TENSE

I walk	we walk
you walk	you walk
he ⎫	
she ⎬ walks	they walk
it ⎭	

PAST TENSE

I walked	we walked
you walked	you walked
he ⎫	
she ⎬ walked	they walked
it ⎭	

FUTURE TENSE

Full Forms

I will walk	we will walk
you will walk	you will walk
he ⎫	
she ⎬ will walk	they will walk
it ⎭	

Contracted Forms

I'll walk	we'll walk
you'll walk	you'll walk
he'll ⎫	
she'll ⎬ walk	they'll walk
it'll ⎭	

PRESENT PERFECT TENSE

Full Forms

I have walked	we have walked
you have walked	you have walked
he ⎫	
she ⎬ has walked	they have walked
it ⎭	

Contracted Forms

I've walked	we've walked
you've walked	you've walked
he's ⎫	
she's ⎬ walked	they've walked
it's ⎭	

PRESENT CONTINUOUS TENSE

Full Forms

I am walking	we are walking
you are walking	you are walking
he ⎫	
she ⎬ is walking	they are walking
it ⎭	

Contracted Forms

I'm walking	we're walking
you're walking	you're walking
he's ⎫	
she's ⎬ walking	they're walking
it's ⎭	

PRINCIPAL PARTS
OF COMMON
IRREGULAR VERBS

Present	Past	Past Participle	Present	Past	Past Participle
be	was, *were*	been	lend	lent	lent
become	became	become	let	let	let
begin	began	begun	lose	lost	lost
blow	blew	blown	make	made	made
bring	brought	brought	mean	meant	meant
build	built	built	meet	met	met
buy	bought	bought	put	put	put
come	came	come	read	read	read
cost	cost	cost	ride	rode	ridden
cut	cut	cut	rise	rose	risen
do	did	done	run	ran	run
draw	drew	drawn	say	said	said
drink	drank	drunk	see	saw	seen
drive	drove	driven	sell	sold	sold
eat	ate	eaten	send	sent	sent
fall	fell	fallen	set	set	set
feel	felt	felt	sing	sang	sung
find	found	found	sit	sat	sat
forget	forgot	forgotten	sleep	slept	slept
get	got	gotten	speak	spoke	spoken
give	gave	given	spend	spent	spent
go	went	gone	stand	stood	stood
grow	grew	grown	swim	swam	swum
hang	hung	hung	take	took	taken
have	had	had	teach	taught	taught
hear	heard	heard	tell	told	told
hurt	hurt	hurt	think	thought	thought
keep	kept	kept	understand	understood	understood
know	knew	known	wear	wore	worn
leave	left	left	write	wrote	written

VOCABULARY

These are words introduced in this book. Each word is followed by a number indicating the lesson in which it first appeared. The words in each lesson are grouped at the end of that lesson under *New Words*. Verbs are indicated as follows: (v) = verb.

a 1
about 34
above 10
absent 24
accountant 7
across 18
actor 41
actress 41
add 22
addition 22
address 36
a few 29
after 23
afternoon 27
airplane 3
airport 38
algebra 19
all 24
alone 34
a lot 19
already 40
always 12
am 7
A.M. 23
an 3
and 7
angry 25
animal 12
answer 27
answer (v) 27
anywhere 28
apartment 35
appear 43
apple 3

appliance 44
appointment 27
April 43
are 4
area 44
aren't 8
arm 3
around 27
arrive 23
artist 9
ask 26
ask for 21
assistant 27
astronaut 37
August 33
aunt 38
autumn 43

bad 8
bag 32
banana 9
barbecue 17
bare 43
baseball 19
bathroom 41
bathtub 44
beach 35
beautiful 24
because 25
bed 44
bedroom 41
before 40
begin 18
behind 10

belong to 17
best 33
better 32
between 10
be worth 23
bicycle 13
big 6
bill 26
biology 37
bird 4
black 6
blackboard 5
blossom (v) 43
blow (v) 40
boat 5
book 4
bookcase 26
boot 2
both 13
bottle 29
bowl 10
box 4
break (v) 39
boy 10
breakfast 12
bring 27
brother 21
brush (v) 34
buckle 17
build 26
bunch 38
burn (v) 36
bus 4
business 36

busy 27
butter 18
button 4
buy 16
by 13 1

cabinet 44
cafeteria 27
calculator 4
calendar 43
camp 16
car 5
care 36
careful 31
carpenter 26
carpet 39
cat 1
catch (v) 31
cent 23
chair 1
change 43
cheese 28
chemistry 38
cherry 21
chess 32
chicken 9
child 10
chocolate 13
circle 33
city 12
class 18
clean 8
clean (v) 37
client 27
clock 23
close (v) 19
closed 6
closet 44
clothes 37
coat 2
coffee 12
coin 23

cold 8
comb (v) 34
come 27
computer 1
computer programmer 9
cook 25
cook(v) 14
cookie 14
cool 43
corner 27
correct 31
cousin 24
cross (v) 39
cry (v) 19
cut (v) 36

dance (v) 20
dancer 9
date 41
day 12
December 43
describe 43
dentist 9
desk 2
dessert 37
dictionary 4
different 23
difficult 32
dime 23
dining room 11
dinner 13
dirty 8
dish 17
dishwasher 19
disk 17
divide 22
division 22
do 12
doctor 7
do dishes 40
dog 1
dollar 23

door 5
down 20
Dr. 9
draw 31
drawer 10
dress 1
dresser 41
drink 28
drink (v) 12
drive (v) 12
driver 25
dry 6
during 23

ear 3
early 31
earring 3
easy chair 44
eat 12
egg 3
eight 18
eighteen 22
eighty 22
electric 17
electrician 18
elephant 3
eleven 22
eleventh 22
else 21
empty 6
end (v) 23
enjoy (v) 26
envelope 3
equal 22
evening 12
ever 42
every 12
exam 31
except 43
expensive 33
explain 19
eye 3

itself 36

January 33
job 25
juice 41
July 33
June 43
just 40

keep 44
key 10
kitchen 11
knife 11
know 14

lamp 4
land (v) 40
large 32
last 24
late 9
lately 40
later 34
laugh (v) 19
laundry 39
lawyer 8
lay 26
lazy 39
leaf 40
leap year 43
learn 19
least 33
leave 23
lecture 26
lend 26
less 32
lesson 19
let (v) 39
letter 5
library 20
lift (v) 36
like (v) 12
linen 44

lion 32
listen to 26
little 6
live (v) 12
living room 41
local 27
long 6
lose 43
loud 31
lunch 13

magazine 19
mail 12
mailbox 5
mail carrier 9
make 23
man 7
manager 42
March 43
market 40
May 43
me 16
meal 39
meat 14
mechanic 7
meet 35
meeting 26
message 27
metal 23
microwave oven 44
midnight 23
milk 14
milkshake 17
mind (v) 39
mine 17
mineral water 29
minus 22
minute 41
mirror 36
Miss 9
Monday 24
money 16

month 33
more 32
morning 12
most 33
mother 16
mountain 37
mouse 13
movies 12
Mr. 9
Mrs. 9
Ms. 9
multiplication 22
multiply 22
music 27
musician 9
my 17
myself 36

name 18
name (v) 43
napkin 11
narrow 33
natural 43
near 20
need (v) 35
never 42
newspaper 2
next 34
nickel 23
night 12
nine 18
nineteen 22
ninety 22
no 2
noon 13
north 32
not 2
notebook 20
novel 40
now 19
November 43
nurse 9